Fascism in the Middle East

Following decades of brutal campaigns against left forces, fascism in its nationalist and religious forms has been dominating Turkish, Iranian, and Arab politics for over half a century. At first, with key enemies vanquished, military generals assumed power and established some of the most terroristic totalitarian regimes in the twentieth century. It only followed that Islamist organizations then hijacked democratic movements of dissent. Now, in countries and territories where they have assumed state power, Islamist forces have surpassed all nationalist dictatorships for their utter disrespect of human lives.

Today, Islamism subordinates peoples in the Middle East. Bearing the urgency of our times, Saladdin Bahozde problematizes all forms of fascist exclusionism in the region, while drawing attention to anti-fascist resistance and progressive alternatives there. As a critique of identitarianism and right-wing politics in the Middle East and North Africa, the work calls for a global movement, as endorsed by the peoples of the region, to go beyond nationalism and Islamism.

Saladdin Bahozde's other books include *The Death of Home* (2024), *Critical Theory from the Margins* (2023), *Revolutionary Hope After Nihilism* (2022), and *Totalitarian Space and the Destruction of Aura* (2019).

Routledge Focus on Modern Subjects

Series Editor: Saurabh Dube, Professor-Researcher, Distinguished Category, El Colegio de México, Mexico City

The volumes in this Focus series explore quotidian claims made on the modern – understood as idea and image, practice and procedure – as part of everyday articulations of modernity in South Asia, Africa, and the Middle East. Here, the category-entity of the subject refers not only to social actors who have been active participants in historical processes of modernity, but as equally implying branch of learning and area of study, topic and theme, question and matter, and issue and business. Our effort is to explore such modern subjects in a range of distinct yet overlaying ways.

The titles in the series address earlier understandings of the modern and recent reconsiderations of modernity by focusing on a clutch of common and critical questions. Indeed, the bid is to carefully query aggrandizing representations of modernity "as" the West, while prudently tracking the place of such projections in the commonplace unravelling of the modern in Global Souths today.

Books in this series include

Disciplines of Modernity
Archives, Histories, Anthropologies
Saurabh Dube

Fluid Modernity
The Politics of Water in the Middle East
Gilberto Conde

Fascism in the Middle East
Nationalism, Islamism, and Imagining Other Futures
Saladdin Bahozde

For more information about this series and its titles, please visit: www.routledge.com/Routledge-Focus-on-Modern-Subjects/book-series/RFOMS.

Fascism in the Middle East

Nationalism, Islamism, and Imagining Other Futures

Saladdin Bahozde

LONDON AND NEW YORK

First published 2025
by Routledge
4 Park Square, Milton Park, Abingdon, Oxon OX14 4RN

and by Routledge
605 Third Avenue, New York, NY 10158

Routledge is an imprint of the Taylor & Francis Group, an informa business

British Library Cataloguing-in-Publication Data
A catalogue record for this book is available from the British Library

Library of Congress Cataloging-in-Publication Data
A catalog record has been requested for this book

ISBN: 978-1-032-39800-6 (hbk)
ISBN: 978-1-032-39801-3 (pbk)
ISBN: 978-1-003-35142-9 (ebk)

DOI: 10.4324/9781003351429

Typeset in Times New Roman
by Taylor & Francis Books

Contents

Series Editor's Statement

Saurabh Dube

Routledge Focus on Modern Subjects has a broad yet particular purpose. It seeks to explore quotidian claims made on the *modern* – understood as idea and image, practice and procedure – as part of everyday articulations of modernity in South Asia, the Middle East, and Africa. Here, the category-entity of the *subject* also has wide purchase. It refers not only to social actors who have been active participants in historical processes of modernity, but equally implies branch of learning and area of study, topic and theme, question and matter, and issue and business. The series attempts to address such modern subjects in a range of distinct yet overlaying ways.

Questions of modernity have always been bound to issues of being/becoming modern. These themes have been discussed in various ways for a long time now.[1] For convenience, we might distinguish between two broad, opposed tendencies. On the one hand, over the past few centuries, it is the West/Europe that has been seen as the locus and the habitus of the modern and modernity. Such a West is imaginary yet tangible, principally envisioned in the image of the North Atlantic world. And it is from these arenas that modernity and the modern appear as spreading outwards to transform other, distant and marginal, peoples in the mould and the wake of the West. On the other hand, such propositions have been contested by rival claims, including especially from within Romanticist and anti-modernist dispositions. Here, if the modern and modernity have been often understood as intimating the fundamental fall of humanity, everywhere, so too have the aggrandizements of an analytical reason been countered through procedures of a hermeneutic provenance.

Needless to say, these contending tendencies have for long each found imaginative articulations, and I provide indicative examples from our own times. The work of philosophers such as Jürgen Habermas and Charles Taylor and historians such as Reinhart

Koselleck and Hans Ulrich Gumbrecht have opened up the exact terms, textures, and transformations of modernity and the modern. At the same time, they have arguably located the constitutive conditions of these phenomenon in Western Europe and Euro-America. In contrast, anti-modernist sensibilities have found innovative elaborations in, say, the "critical traditionalism" of Ashis Nandy in South Asia; and the querying of Eurocentric thought has been intriguingly expressed by the scholars of the "coloniality of knowledge" and "decoloniality of power" in Latin America. These powerful positions variously rest on assumptions of innocence before and outside Europe and the West, modernity and the modern.

Engaging with, yet going beyond such prior emphases, recent work on modernity has charted new directions, departures that have served to foreground questions of modernity in academic agendas and on intellectual horizons, more broadly. I indicate four critical trends. First and foremost, there have been works focusing on different expressions of the modern and distinct articulations of modernity as historically grounded and/or culturally expressed, articulations that query *a priori* projections and sociological formalisms underpinning the category-entity. Second, there are the studies that have diversely explored issues of "early" and "colonial" and "multiple" and "alternative" modernity/modernities. Third, we find imaginative ethnographic, historical, and theoretical explorations of modernity's conceptual cognates such as globalization, capitalism, and cosmopolitanism as well as of attendant issues of state, nation, and democracy. Fourth and finally, there have been varied explorations of the enchantments of modernity and of the magic of the modern, understood not as analytical errors but as formative of social worlds. These studies have ranged from the elaborations of the fetish of the state, the sacred character of modern sovereignty, the uncanny of capitalism, and the routine enticements of modernity through to the secular magic of representational practices such as entertainment shows, cinema, and advertising.

Routledge Focus on Modern Subjects engages and exceeds, takes forward and departs from such concerns in its own manner. To start off, its titles address the queries and concepts entailed in earlier explorations of the modern and recent reconsiderations of modernity by focusing on a clutch of common and critical questions. These issues turn on the everyday elaborations of the modern, the quotidian configurations of modernity, in South Asia, Africa, and the Middle East. Next, rather than simply asserting the empirical plurality of modernity and the modern, the series approaches the routine, even banal, expressions of the modern as registering contingency, contradiction, and contention as lying at the core of modernity. Further, it only follows that our bid is not to indolently exorcize aggrandizing representations of modernity *as* the West, but to prudently track instead the play of such projections in the commonplace unravelling of the modern in Global Souths today. Finally, such procedures not only recast broad questions – for instance of cosmopolitanism and globalization, state and citizenship, Eurocentrism and Nativism, aesthetics and authority – by approaching them through routine renderings of the modern in contemporary Africa, South Asia, and the Middle East. They also stay with the dense, exact expressions of modernity yet all the while attending to their larger, critical implications, prudently thinking *both* down to the ground.

In keeping with the spirit of the series, all its titles stand informed by specific renderings – as well as focused rethinking – of key categories and processes. Two exact instances. In different ways, concepts and procedures of power and politics alongside those of community and identity variously run through the *Focus Series on Modern Subjects*. Here, neither power nor politics are rendered as signifying solely institutional relations of authority centring on the state and its subjects. Rather, the bid is to articulate these as equally embodying diffuse domains and intimate arrangements of authority and desire, including their seductions and subversions. Actually, as parts of such force-fields, state and government, their policy and program might now assume twinned dimensions in understandings of modern subjects. Here can be found densely embodied disciplinary techniques toward forming and transforming subjects-citizens, where such protocols and their reworking by citizens-subjects no less intimate the following twinned registers: the shaping of authority by anxiety, uncertainty, and alterity; and of the structuring of command by deferral, difference, and displacement.

At the same time, the series approaches community and identity as modern processes of meaning and authority, located at core of nation and globalization. This is to say that instead of approaching identity and community as already given entities that are principally antithetical to modernity, this cluster explores communities and identities as wide-ranging processes of formations of subjects, expressing collective groupings and particular personhoods. Defined within social relationships of production and reproduction, appropriation and approbation, and power and difference, emergent identities, cultural communities, and their mutations appear now as essential elements in the quotidian constitution, expressions, and transformations of modern subjects.

The Book

Saladdin Bahozde's *Fascism in the Middle East* (henceforth *FME*) incisively articulates the desire of *Routledge Focus on Modern Subjects* to widen the address of modernity and its subjects. On the one hand, the book joins Gilberto Conde's *Fluid Modernity* in extending the locus of the series to the Middle Eastern world, expanding its prior focus on South Asia. On the other hand, Saladdin seizes upon distinct "modern subjects" that entail equally "subjects of modernity"[2]: the politics and cultures – indeed, the political cultures and cultural politics – of fascism, nationalism, Islamism, and glimmers of alternative futures in the Middle East. These fraught formations ever draw in the interests and energies of wider worlds. Together, it is the interleaving of these twinned imperatives that exemplify the compelling mutuality of *FME* and *Routledge Focus on Modern Subjects* – including the necessity to think, search, and grope outside-the-box.

Saladdin is a courageous author-thinker-philosopher and *FME* is a brave book. This is evident from the very start of the work. Its opening explorations showcase an acutely critical imagination and sensibility as well as a formidable fortitude of commitment and conviction, while interleaving these with a biting sense of play and humour. Here, Saladdin explores the power-politics of naming, especially of the "Middle East" as a category and entity, by conjoining these considerations with moving pasts of his own "no-name name."

Let me turn to the words of our intrepid author:

> In Iraq, a set of identities and names were imposed on me. Even my birth name, Scherzad, was changed to Saladdin precisely not to draw any attention to my Kurdish identity … [such that] my official (Arabized) name was alienating, to say the least. … Saladdin, to me, signifies the denial of Scherzad. Ahmed, which became my last name by default, was my paternal grandfather's first name, about whose life and death I know very little. My name was the antipathy of a proper name because it functioned as a non-indicator or an indicator of a wordless being lacking subjectivity. It denoted colonialism on a personal level. It was meant to refer to nothing in particular, to denote nobody or a nobody. Namelessness, therefore, has always been both personal and political for me. … After publishing my seventh book, at the age of fifty-one, I finally decided to choose a last name and leave "Ahmed" in peace. All that to say, I started problematizing the idea of identity from an early age … and now I would say that

> problem has been ontological and political throughout. Is my affinity with the marginalized rooted in my own sense of namelessness? Or my sense of namelessness stems from my deep affinity with the marginalized? I have no reliable knowledge about that but … I have always identified with the nameless, the outcast, and the marginalized, and my affinity has always been with otherness and elsewhereness. Kurdishness gave a great deal of negative satisfaction not as the condition of being othered but as a politicized ground for otherness and for rejecting the existing order. As soon as I witnessed Kurdishness being enacted as a privilege, I took an oppositional position against it, siding with those whom it minoritized.
>
> (Chapter 1, p. 3–4)

It is in these ways that, in Saladdin's hands, the "naming" of the Middle East and its subjects – as well as of course of wider worlds and their beings and non-beings – appear as "part of the industry of identities, which is controlled by the privileged elites while its products are consumed by the majority."

I have taken the liberty of quoting at some length from *FME* not only to introduce the author's emphases but to announce his particular persona. Needless to say, there is much that I have learnt from the present work as well as from Saladdin as an intensely human subject. But none of this was readily all of a piece. Actually, after receiving two stellar reports from anonymous reviewers, both experts on the Middle East, it was myself, the layman series editor, who initiated a process of revisiting, rethinking, and rewriting of the work. All of this involved extended interchanges over several months with Saladdin over email and Zoom. These conversations – full of laughter and life, the intellectual and the everyday – have left me all the richer as they have the book and its arguments.

And it is exactly for these reasons that rather than writing the usual Foreword to the volumes in this series, I offer only this short statement. For, I have come to realize how little I understand about the terrains, terms, and textures of politics of the Middle East – not only their knowing but their unknowing – that *FME* traverses. And so, I now invite you, the reader, to embark with Saladdin on an extraordinary journey: intense treks across spaces and politics of fascism and identity, nationalism and Islamism, prior and emergent alternatives and movements – all this over vast swathes of "West Asia", known to us as the Middle East, each turning upon the politics of naming.

Notes

1 The discussion in this Statement of different understandings of modernity (and the modern) draws upon a wide range of scholarship. Instead of cluttering the short piece with numerous references, indicated here are a few of my works that have addressed these themes – in dialogue with relevant literatures – and that back the claims made ahead. Needless to say, prior arguments and emphases are being cryptically condensed and radically rearranged for the present purposes. Saurabh Dube, *Subjects of Modernity: Time/Space, Disciplines, Margins* (Manchester: Manchester University Press, 2017); Saurabh Dube, *Stitches on Time: Colonial Textures and Postcolonial Tangles* (Durham and London: Duke University Press, 2004); and Saurabh Dube, *Disciplines of Modernity: Archives, Histories, Anthropologies* (London and New Delhi: Routledge, 2023). Consider also, Saurabh Dube, *After Conversion: Cultural Histories of Modern India* (New Delhi: Yoda Press, 2010), Saurabh Dube (ed.), *Enchantments of Modernity: Empire, Nation, Globalization* (New Delhi and London: Routledge, 2009, 2010); and Saurabh Dube (ed.), *Handbook of Modernity in South Asia: Modern Makeovers* (New Delhi: Oxford University Press, 2011).

2 For the distinction between "modern subjects" and "subjects of modernity" see especially Dube, *Subjects of Modernity.*

Acknowledgments

First and foremost, I am grateful to Saurabh Dube, the Editor of *Routledge Focus of Modern Subjects* and author of, among an extensive list of volumes, *Disciplines of Modernity* (2023) for placing his confidence in the project and working so selflessly to ensure the best possible outcome. After successfully facilitating the review process, he patiently reviewed several versions of the manuscript providing rounds of helpful feedback up until the last stage. In addition to providing detailed written comments on the earlier versions of the manuscript, Saurabh generously spared more time for two extremely constructive and pleasant online meetings to help me plan and execute necessary revisions. Saurabh's persisting commitment as a series editor and an intellectual interlocutor resulted in a substantially more focused manuscript.

Many thanks to Towfeeq Wani, Commissioning Editor at Routledge, for his continual and kind assistance throughout the pre-production stages. Thanks to Amrita Sood and Aafreen Ayub as well for their helpful contributions in different stages of the process. I am also immensely grateful to everyone who worked behind the scenes to convert the digital document into the living breathing entity called a book. I salute them and express my deepest appreciation for their collaborative and creative labor.

Gilberto Conde, the Middle East specialist and author of *Fluid Modernity* (2022), an invaluable book on water politics in the Middle East, read an earlier version of the manuscript and shared much-appreciated thoughts about it. I sincerely thank him for that and his continued collegiality and support over the years. I also send my sincere thanks to the peer reviewers for their conducting close readings of the manuscript and writing supportive comments and constructive recommendations. Judith Friedlander patiently read and commented on what later became parts of the manuscript. I met Judith and the

Director of the New University in Exile Consortium, Arien Mack, in late 2019 in New York. Since then, they have been strongly supporting my academic career. I sincerely thank them for their limitless collegiality and solidarity.

Some parts of the book are based on previously published articles and commentaries; I appreciate the republication permissions by the respective publishers. Parts of the discussion about Hamas and the Gaza war are based on two pieces. One of them was titled, “Turkey: Erdogan’s 2023 neo-Ottoman imperialist agenda, from the Caucasus to the Mediterranean” and was published on October 19, 2023, by LINKS, the International Journal for Socialist Renewal, based in Australia. The other one was titled “The ‘Jerusalem Flood’ and Erdogan’s Caliphate Project: The Islamist Reconquista as a Doomsday for Palestinians,” posted by Eurasia Review on November 5, 2023.

Chapter 3 is mainly based on an article titled, “Exclusionary Politics (or Fascism) in the Middle East.” The article appeared in *New Political Science* issue 45, number 3, in June 2023. I appreciate the republication permission by Taylor & Francis. Also, my appreciation goes to the journal’s editorial staff and the peer reviewers who provided valuable comments. Some parts of Chapter 3 also draw on an article titled “Fascism is Alive and Well,” a Turkish translation of which was published in issue 21 of the journal of *Demokratik Modernite* in 2017. My gratitude to the Editor, Servet Öner, the rest of the journal’s staff, and the translator/s.

Many thanks to Samir Gandesha, the Director of the Institute for the Humanities at Simon Fraser University, for permitting me to republish my article, “The Left’s Culturalism and Rojava,” which was originally published in the Institute’s issue 9 of *Contours Journal* in 2019. Some parts of Chapter 4 are based on that article. Finally, I must add that I highly value Samir’s continual and generous support over many years.

1 Abyss or Eclipse of Leftism

The expression "the Middle East" was manufactured by European elites towards the end of the nineteenth century and started to gain currency about 100 years ago to indicate a region visa vie, of course, Europe. In reference to the parts of Asia that were closer to Europe than the parts that are called "the Far East," we also see the uses of "the Near East" starting in the end of the 1800s and increasing in the 1900s. Over the last 100 years, the region that is designated as the Middle East has been falsely imagined as if it were not part of Asia. It should go without saying that, geographically, "West Asia and North Africa" would be more accurate than "the Middle East and North Africa," but the label MENA has more to do with the dominant racist and culturalist mode of perception than geography per se. That said, there is hardly any such thing as geography per se in the dominant knowledge system. In a world that has been mapped, divided, colonized, and exploited according to the capitalist modes of spatial production, geography is not saved from the distortions of the epistemology that is at work in the other fields of knowledge, including biology. Once geographic perception is shaped around the dominant *model of power*, or, per Quijano, *coloniality*, then human history, like social geography, is naturalized racially. "The Middle East" is first and foremost a construct within coloniality, and the inhabitants of the region are, therefore, reduced to the negative shadow of the European man's assumed Other. Within the region itself, that shadow has been positivized and, sometimes tragically and sometimes farcically, reproduced thereby ontologizing *race*, which is at the heart of *coloniality as a model of power.*[1]

DOI: 10.4324/9781003351429-1

On the Terminologies and the Political Economy of Naming: A Critique of Identitarianism

The power of naming is part of domination. The dominant names and in doing so reduces people's worlds, views, politics, etc., to their subject positions. The colonialist goes much further by imposing material conditions that are meant to subjugate the colonized subjects. The ensuing political economy of naming assigns identities that transcendentalize subversion denying the members of the collectively named personhood. The result of coloniality for the colonized is far more severe than the reduction to the subjective position; rhetorically, it is annihilation, which is a step toward normalizing physical annihilation. Meanwhile, those who are dominated cannot name as long as the historical and social conditions that are imposed on them endure. They cannot name themselves or choose their identities as long as they are dominated. Renaming things, places, and selves may be of some symbolic significance, but it is pure idealism to conflate attempts of renaming with actual transformation in social relations of power.

Lumping the peoples of the region together under the term MENA was the Eurocentric way to designate the area inhabited by Arabs, and, therefore, the geographic core of the so-called Muslim world. The Arab-Muslim identity, which has also been conflated with the Moor, has become the assumed Other of the European Christian since the Crusaders. Indeed, the veterans of *Reconquista* were so obsessed with this figure that some among those who went on to colonize the Americas insisted that the Aztecs were Moors, citing not only costumes, traditional dances, and facial features of the Aztecs but also the architectural styles to prove their claim! Cortés went as far as claiming that he personally had seen about 400 mosques in present-day Mexico (Mikhail 2020, chapter 8).

Although I would prefer to use "West Asia" instead of "Middle East," in this book, I will stick with the problematic term as I try to problematize its present state as a historical moment caught up between oppressive global and regional powers pushing large numbers of people within the impoverished demographics into the production and reproduction of violence. I will use the term the Middle East to also name the naming process and critique the hegemonic homogenizing enterprises. To name is seldom, if ever, to identify. Naming is part of the industry of identities, which is controlled by the privileged elites while its products are consumed by the majority.

Geographically, while not always clear in terms of boundaries, the meaning of "the Middle East" is known, but what does it mean to be a Middle Eastern? I, for one, at least before migrating to Canada, would identify as an Asian, as a matter of truism, in geographic terms. It was, and I believe still is, unheard of for people to be identified as "Middle Eastern" in any of the countries I lived or traveled through. That is certainly not to say domination, including the power to name, was not a problem where I grew up. On the contrary, at work is a much more complex picture of colonialisms, imperialisms, classifications, namings, and politics of identities, than the Eurocentrically imagined picture of the region.

In Iraq, a set of identities and names were imposed on me. Even my birth name, Scherzad, was changed to Saladdin precisely not to draw any attention to my Kurdish identity in Kirkuk, a multi-ethnic ancient city that, decades before I was born, became the main issue of nationalist conflicts among several movements. By the 1970s, it had already become the major dispute between the pan-Arab government of Al-Baath Party and the pan-Kurdish movement led by Mustafa Barzani. Being born into a Kurdish working family in Kirkuk amounted to a political start up in life, and a potentially nasty one at that. Thus, my official (Arabized) name was alienating, to say the least.

To make things worse for this peculiarity in a world that was not especially welcoming for the racially minoritized and spatially marginalized underclass youth, I refused to take my relatives' last name because I did not want to identify on what I considered to be clannist basis, especially because my family's family name indicated a social status of superiority, which, given my egalitarian and secular inclinations, did not sit well with me, to put it mildly. Having been denied my first name and having denied myself a family name, I ended up with an even less unique name. Saladdin, to me, signifies the denial of Scherzad. Ahmed, which became my last name by default, was my paternal grandfather's first name, about whose life and death I know very little. My name was the antipathy of a proper name because it functioned as a non-indicator or an indicator of a worldless being lacking subjectivity. It denoted colonialism on a personal level. It was meant to refer to nothing in particular, to denote nobody or a nobody. Namelessness, therefore, has always been both personal and political for me.

At any rate, every time I published something (first in Kurdish and Arabic, and since my mid-thirties in English as well) I used some form of my no-name name. Sometimes, I also used a penname for a couple of pieces before abandoning it. After publishing my seventh book, at the age of 51, I finally decided to choose a last name and leave

"Ahmed" in peace. All that to say, I started problematizing the idea of identity from an early age because of personal and social, individual and political, geographic and historical, circumstances. I have not heard my relatives complaining about their names, but in my case naming has been a problem, and now I would say that problem has been ontological and political throughout. Is my affinity with the marginalized rooted in my own sense of namelessness? Or my sense of namelessness stems from my deep affinity with the marginalized? I have no reliable knowledge about that, but I do not think the answer matters anyway because, at the end of the day, every human in the world comes from multifaceted histories and social spaces and with an inner black box with undeterminable properties in terms of the ways in which it processes the social environment and engages in worlding the world for one's self and others.

For better or worse, I have always identified with the nameless, the outcast, and the marginalized, and my affinity has always been with otherness and elsewhereness. Kurdishness gave a great deal of negative satisfaction not as the condition of being othered but as a politicized ground for otherness and for rejecting the existing order. As soon as I witnessed Kurdishness being enacted as a privilege, I took an oppositional position against it, siding with those whom it minoritized. That was the case in 2013–2014, when I taught at the University of Duhok in Iraqi Kurdistan, and for the first time witnessed Kurds acting from a position of power and privilege toward not only non-Kurds but also Kurdish refugees who had been relocated from Syria due to the Syrian civil war.

All my published work has to do with critique. While my English publications may give the impression that I focus on the critique of the West, I have to mention that my Kurdish and Arabic publications are centered around the critique of Kurdish and Arab majority societies, respectively. To borrow the wording from Leo Lowenthal, "as a good Marxist I acted according to the principle of beginning with criticism at home" (1987, 117). This is my first book on the Middle East in English, but like the rest of my books, whether in English, Arabic, or Kurdish, it does not try to win any particular ethnic or religious group's appraisal. On the contrary, it is meant to be a critique of exclusionism of all sides, and the critique starts from home. That is to say, this book aims to be critical of the dominant and internalized right-wing ideologies in West Asia: nationalism and Islamism. Domination here should be read as hegemony, which is the work of the elites.

The critique goes further than that to question what the editor of the book series Routledge Focus of Modern Subjects, Saurabh Dube, critically calls "modernity 'as' the West" (2023). "Modernity as the West" has assumed, named, and constructed its Others epistemologically and geopolitically. In this context, critiquing hegemony requires thorough processes of deconstructing what Dube calls the "disciplines of modernity," which is the title of his above cited book. The first book in the series on MENA is Gilberto Conde's *Fluid Modernity* (2022). As a historical discussion of hydropolitics, biopolitics, and the intensifying water crisis in MENA, it is an urgently needed contribution.

This book has in common with Dube's *Disciplines of Modernity* and Conde's *Fluid Modernity* the fidelity to what I would call Otherness, not as identity, but as progressive negations and transformative modes of perception. Critical theory as a Marxist intervention in the history of truth-making has been militantly anti-hegemonic, that is, anti-totalitarian in the realms of knowledge production, including the bourgeois separation between theory and practice, history and geography, economics and politics, etc. Critical theory in that sense is a perpetual search for silenced histories and histories of the silenced. Otherwise, it will cease to be a negative praxis in the present moment and, therefore, it will become irrelevant in terms of crystalizing horizons of possibility, which in turn means it will cease to be a critical theory. Taking off from this point, and to avoid the fate of critical theories that have unknowingly joined the totalitarian machine of the assumed post-Marxist world, I will regularly return to the starting point, to the Marxist premises, negations, and negativities.

The means of the production of knowledge have been monopolized by elites whose exclusionary interests and views have produced a mode of perception that is deeply antagonistic to otherness. In today's world, it is easy to be deceived by a discourse of victimhood and conflate the nationalist or sectarian image produced by an elite for the population that is supposedly depicted by that false identity. I say false identity because it is manufactured by a privileged minority and generalized through the production and reproduction of false consciousness. This is one of the direct consequences of the decline of class consciousness, which in turn results in what is called mass politics. However, "mass politics" implies a typical elitist and antidemocratic charge against the marginalized majority, blaming them for the perpetuation of conditions of unfreedom. Therefore, in place of massification, I have suggested mobomassification: the bourgiosification of the underclass through popularizing a mob mentality resulting in identitarianism (see Ahmed 2022a; 2023a).

Identitarianism is disguised tribalism or a mode of perception that homogenizes and transcendentalizes race, sect, nationality, and culture, all of which otherwise should be perceived as mythological constructs invented and reinvented in order to sustain certain modes of production and relations of power. Forms of identitarianism, such as nationalism and culturalism, started to gain unprecedented global hegemony as the doctrine of communism began to lose currency in the 1980s while simultaneously neoliberalism was reshaping the global political economy. In the 1990s, as neoliberalism stormed the administrative vacancy state capitalism had left behind in the former republics of the USSR and the satellite states in Eastern Europe, identitarianism was filling the corresponding ideological void the demise of socialism had caused. Thus, as the twentieth century came to its end, we entered another gloomy age characterized by advanced totalitarianism, that is, the unlimited exercise of the power of capital, while new tribalism, or the disguised racism of culturalism and ethnic nationalism, quickly pushed the entire regime of knowledge production toward an abyss of the war of all against all whereby gods, prophets, scriptures, ethnicities, traditions, dialects, languages, flags, etc. were mobilized as part of the war efforts.

Indeed, if the nine-eleven attacks and the immediate American reaction were any indication, the twenty-first century was set to be a self-fulfillment of one of the worst prophesies of the neoliberal ideology: the Huntingtonian idea of "clash of civilizations." As the first quarter of the century ends, what we witness is indeed the materialization of that nightmare, except civilizations do not clash, barbarians do, and in this case, barbarians have taken over much of the civilization, especially in parts of the world where religious wars were once the norm. To be fair, China has succeeded in staying out of this clash of barbarians, but there are continual efforts to drag it into the conflicts. In the meantime, for much of Africa and Latin America coloniality (per Anibal Quijano 2000), which includes economic subjugations through the use of racist and religious means, has never ended anyway, but the moment of hope that communism created around the mid-twentieth century is also over.

According to the identitarian mode of perception and its corresponding regime of knowledge production, class divisions are almost completely denied in the interest of the noted metaphysicalized and transcendentalized myths and social constructs. Conflicts among ruling groups are popularized, globalized, and naturalized on the basis of nationalism, culturalism, sectarianism, and so on. Perhaps the clearest examples at the present moment are the ongoing conflicts in Russia/Ukraine and Israel/Palestine. While ultra-right-wing elites have dragged the respective populations of those regions into deadly violence, those who benefit from the war industry along with opinion makers elsewhere have succeeded in the deployment of the same identitarian modes of perception across the world. Thus, today, whatever one writes about those conflicts, the first question most of us are trained to search for is, "which side one is taking?" The false consciousness has become the norm, and the totalized regime of falsehood insists on validating or invalidating our intellectual, political, and moral sanity. Thus, there are two camps: those who support Israel versus those who support Palestine, when Israel is used obscurely to mean the state, the country, the government, the Jewish citizens of the country, and/or the Netanyahu cabinet and Palestine is used obscurely to mean those who identify as Palestinians, those who identify as Palestinians and are in one or more of the Palestinian territories occupied by the state of Israel, Palestinian Arabs, Palestinian Muslims, Palestinian Islamists, Palestinian political parties, Palestinian authorities, the Palestinian Arabic speaking residences in the territories and Israel, etc. The obscure terminology is not just relevant here but also an indication of the false mode of perception that is at the heart of identitarianism.

Identitarianism is founded on deceptive lenses and misleading standards precisely in order to depoliticize what is political and politicize what is non-political, to undermine struggles for equality and replace them with conflicts for dominations, to maintain class domination through racializing social relations and perpetuate racial domination through social deployment of class rule. Identitarianism, in short, is a regime of truth and power that metaphysicalizes an already false order and renders the chasm separating the real and the true ever larger. That is precisely what I mean by the fulfillment of a false prophecy. What is realized through falsehood is cited as proof of the truth. This is the principle of realism. But at the same time, what is deduced from prevalent relations of oppression is cited as evidence for the real. This is the principle of empiricism. The production of suffering for the most and privilege for a few is precisely what is meant to be sustained materially through the deployment of idealism. Identitarianism, e.g., culturalism, is the most common tool of idealism that aims to eternalize false consciousness, which in turn ensures the perpetuation of a world of endless exploitation of people and the environment, the endless accumulation of capital as power, the totalitarian exercise of power, all of which translates into limitless violence justifying limitless violence reproducing limitless violence and so on.

When the world is perceived from the perspective of identitarianism, whichever side one takes, one is necessarily wrong because the sides are named on false bases. An Israeli victim of Hamas's aggression and a Palestinian victim of the Israeli right-wing government's aggression have more in common with each other than what either of them might have in common with Palestinian and Israeli right-wing elites. If nothing else, they have suffering in common. But of course, we are always told that someone's suffering is less or more justified than someone else's suffering depending on the identities involved. Also, it is as if the validity of the moral justifications that are presented by opinion makers make suffering for person A more or less justifiable than suffering for person B depending on each party's mother tongue, birthplace, and number of other victims who speak this or that language and are born in this or that location. In short, while the moral sentiment is central in identitarian discourses, the unspoken and unproblematized adoption of the identitarian mode of perception renders standing with the victims impossible.

By now, the reader should have already realized that this book will be critical of his or her political and moral stances. As a critical work, it is more likely to be disliked by the advocates of all sides whether we are talking about politics pertaining Kurds, Persians, Turks, Arabs or Israelis because it is indeed critical of not only elites but also elites' false classifications that have been imposed on societies. In agreement with Saurabh Dube's position regarding the multiplicity of modernity (see Dube 2023), i.e., the argument that there are modernities as opposed to "the modernity," the most critical aspect about this book is that it rejects traditional historicity, the products of which knowingly or unknowingly assume metaphysical perspectives of history. That is to say: 1- the contemporary history of MENA could have taken a very different rout, 2- the history of the present is by no means done, and 3- that history, like any history, is never exhaustible whether in terms of conclusive depictions or plurality of endurances, manifestations, etc.

Therefore, MENA is not one MENA. The MENA I aim to uncover in terms of its history, present, and history of present, is different in its compositions, horizons, and manifestations from the MENA imposed by identitarians. It is a diverse MENA perceived from a non-idealist and an anti-reductive perspective that could help open up the subject matter and our interpretations to a multitude of critical possibilities premised on imperative deconstruction and anti-reductive reconstruction. This book is a critique of the exclusionary MENA that is produced and reproduced by identitarians, including nationalists, Islamists, orientalists, self-orientalists, and culturalists. It critiques both ideological and spatial exclusionism with no mercy, so dominant idealogues in the intelligentsia will inevitably find enough reason to dislike it. For that I offer no apology.

Events, Clashes, and Imperialist Projects

One of the challenges of writing a book about the Middle East politics is that by the time of the publication so much will have happened that the introduction would already feel dated. When I prepared the first version of this book, the Sudanese revolution was ongoing as the only movement of the Arab Spring that had continued resisting both military rule and Islamism. By the time of the last revision process of the manuscript, all hope for a civilian government in Sudan ended as a war broke out between the army led by Abdel Fattah al-Burhan and the Rapid Support Forces, led by Mohamed Hamdan Dagalo, also known as Hemedti. Al-Burhan was a general in Omar Al-Bashir's regime, and Hemedti led the Janjaweed, an Arab militia that, along with the army, committed the genocide against the non-Arab population of Darfur, including the Furs and other native Africans killing hundreds of thousands and displacing millions. The current war between two of the heads of the genocidal machine from Al-Bashir's era has been causing even more destruction and mass displacement in Darfur and other areas, including Khartoum and Omdurman.

When I was preparing the manuscript for a review process, there was an uprising taking place in Iran, which was triggered by soaring fuel prices. After the completion of the review process, that revolution had been suppressed, but the Mehsa Jina Amini revolution was at its peak in Iran. Amini was killed by the morality police in September 2022, and the incident triggered one of the most popular uprisings against the regime. Another year on, the Iranian regime has suppressed the Amini revolution and killed hundreds of peaceful protesters.

Under the current regime in Tehran, Iran stood out in another relevant matter: it became the only state that condemned awarding the Noble Price to one of its citizens, Narges Mohammedi, who is the second Iranian human rights activist to receive the prize. She has been arrested repeatedly and convicted by the Islamic Republic's courts five times. She has been in prison in the notorious Even prison after she was arrested last time for attending a commemoration of the Mehsa Jina Amini. Twenty years ago, the human rights activist and former judge, Shirin Abadi won the prize. Facing continual harassment by the regime, in 2009, Abadi left Iran and has been living in exile since then. Both Shirin Abadi and Narges Mohammedi are among the leading figures of the Defenders of Human Rights Center. The same regime, in the name of resisting Americanism and Zionism has created militia run proxy states in Iraq, Lebanon, and Yemen while Erdogan's Turkey has been trying to do a similar thing in the region as part of Erdogan's Caliphate project.

The Hamas attack of October 7, 2023, was the beginning of a bloodier age, the self-fulfilling prophecy of both Islamists and Huntingtonians. Of course, I am alluding to the so-called "clash of civilizations," which is compatible with the Islamist notion of war between the so-called "nation of Islam" and its alleged enemies. However, to reiterate, civilizations do not clash, and there is no such thing as "nation of Islam." What we have been witnessing is a conflict of exclusionary and expansionist forces, where ordinary people are sacrificed on such scales that entire populations are then dragged into the conflicts. Hamas's role and – what in my view are – false justifications of its acts as a form of resistance only further condition the world for racial and sectarian violence conducted through the most advanced technologies available.

I think Hamas's attack was part of a broader religious crusade to mark 2023 as the beginning of the neo-Ottoman Empire. For years, Islamists in Turkey have been bragging about Erdogan's plan to wipe out their enemies and announce a new Ottoman Empire in 2023. During the last two weeks of September and the first week of October, a series of events took the world by surprise. Even for the Middle East, so many events in such a short period of time are not normal. Rather than assuming they are coincidences, we can easily diagnose their common denominator: Erdogan's Turkey. In Nagorno-Karabakh and northern Syria, the Turkish government did not hide the fact that it was a main player. However, because Erdogan knew that Turkey's involvement in any attack on Israel would not be viewed by his Western allies as just another regional dispute in which Turkey violates international treaties, invades other countries, and forcibly displaces populations on nationalist, ethnic, or religious bases, any potential involvement must have been clandestine.

While rarely allusions to a possible link between Turkey and Hamas's attack on Israel are made in the Media, it is more than reasonable to search for such a link. Turkey has been the main base for Hamas's leadership outside Gaza as well as for numerous other Islamist leaders, from the heads of the Egyptian and Syrian Muslim Brotherhood to those of organizations that have tens of thousands of jihadi fighters in Syria, Libya, and beyond. Today, Islamism is more dangerous than ever because it has a global capital where its strategies are planned and coordinated. The Hamas attack seems to have been designed to conclude 2023 by fulfilling one of the most central promises of Islamism: the takeover of Jerusalem. Turkish Islamists had been pointing to 2023 as the year of the fulfillment of their most important objective: the revival of the Ottoman Empire, the caliphate that would enforce its old territorial borders.[2]

Let us first revisit what happened in the weeks leading to October 7. Nagorno-Karabakh fell under Azerbaijani control, forcing the entire Armenian population to leave. Internationally Nagorno-Karabakh is considered to be part of the Azerbaijani state, but international recognition of a state's sovereignty over a territory has previously been used by states to commit genocide, as occurred for example in South Sudan (before its independence), Darfur, Kurdistan, Rakhine, and Tigray. The accepted norms of international relations often obscure rights of minority peoples and international laws systematically disadvantage those racialized and dehumanized by the ruling groups of nation-states. Nationalist ruling groups often use ultranationalist and fundamentalist discourses to prepare ethnic majorities for legitimizing genocidal state politics. This is especially the case in MENA, where, as Chapter 2 in this book explains, fascism is yet to be problematized and denialism (of past and ongoing genocides) is the norm rather than the exception.

With Ankara's support, and Moscow's implicit complicity, the regime in Baku launched an attack in September 2023 putting an end to Artsakh and forcing more than 150,000 Armenians to flee their homes. Azerbaijani president Ilham Aliyev and Erdogan shamelessly paraded themselves as victors in the war against the Armenians of Nagorno-Karabakh, who had been living under a blockade imposed following a previous Azerbaijani attack, with the direct support of Turkey, in 2022 that ended with Azerbaijan seizing control of the Lachin corridor. To anyone who followed the Azerbaijani military campaigns in 2022 and 2023, it was abundantly clear that Turkish drones and warfare expertise made the decisive difference. Thus, one hundred years after the mass killing and displacement of Armenians in what is now Turkey, Turkish nationalism again went to war against a defenseless Armenian population, under near-complete international silence. In Turkey, any affirmative mention of the Armenian genocide is punishable by law; non denialism, as opposed to denialism, is banned. This is a symptom of the continuation of the project of genocide, or at least genocidal tendencies. The dominant politics in MENA showcase this point: Arab nationalism, for example in Sudan; Turkish nationalism, for example in Rojava; and various versions of Islamism across MENA continually reaffirm this.

Around the same time of the surprise attack on Nagorno-Karabakh and the following weeks in late September and early October 2023, the Turkish government intensified its attacks against Rojava and the areas under the control of the multi-ethnic Syrian Democratic Forces (SDF).[3] In early September, some Arab tribes in the east (especially in the Deir ez-Zor province, most of which is under SDF rule) and in the eastern towns of Aleppo (such as Jarablus, run by Turkish-backed Syrian Islamist groups) declared jihad against the Kurds and targeted the SDF positions. The Turkish government continually tries to create a civil war between Arabs and Kurds to instigate an ethnic cleansing of Kurds in Rojava (Ashdown 2020; Boyle 2023). The religious and tribal mobilization among some Sunni Arab tribes in parts of Iraq and Syria in 2023 was especially alarming. Most of those tensions were successfully contained by the SDF. With plans for instigating a wide-scale ethnic war failing, immediately after those events, Turkey escalated its threats on Rojava. Indeed, Human Rights Watch asserted that between October 5 and 10, 2023, Turkey further escalated its attacks on Rojava targeting water and electricity infrastructure in about 150 locations across the areas of the Autonomous Administration of North and East Syria (HRW 2023).

Erdogan sees the political aspirations of Kurds as an obstacle to his pan-Turkic and Islamic empire, but that is not all. A caliphate – the ultimate goal of all Islamists – would not be complete without Jerusalem. Erdogan, like every other Islamist leader, has been capitalizing on anti-Semitism but in his own pragmatic way. Targeting the state of Israel might have been strategized within the neo-Ottoman project, which also explains the exploitation of the Palestinian plight by Islamists.

However, even if Turkey's involvement is uncovered by Western states' intelligence services, it is naïve to think the information will be made public. It is doubtful that the US intelligence does not have sufficient information showing Turkey's direct responsibility for the rise of ISIS, yet the topic remains widely hushed. Turkey's rulers, like those of Qatar, have been playing a double-sided game: on the one hand, supporting Islamist groups; on the other hand, leveraging their indispensable role as mediators between Islamist groups and interested parties in the West.

One of the critical issues that is relevant to the core of this book is the false moral arguments that are used to portray Islamist forces' acts as some sort of legitimate resistance. Referring to the frustration of Gazans to justify Hamas's acts makes such an apologetic position worse because Gazans themselves, including Hamas's sympathizers and the youth who became Hamas followers because of and through a combination of material desperation and ideological deception, are systematically used as hostages by Hamas's leadership. Islamists are a small minority, but they have too many enablers. In the MENA region, some people's failure to realize that Islamist movements, such as Hamas and Hezbollah, represent right-wing movements of the worst kind likely originates from sheer frustration in the age of the demise of emancipatory and egalitarian movements in the region and beyond.

For Islamism's apologists in the West, the failure to recognize that Islamist parties are ultra-right-wing movements is likely to be rooted in a racist mentality that is incapable of conceiving a non-white society as politically diverse, with internal right-wing and left-wing, fascist and anti-fascist, oppressive and emancipatory forces, potentialities and conflicts. A mentality that normally considers Islamism to be the general worldview of any society is deeply immersed in a racist mode of perception. In case the fallacy I am alluding to is unclear let me add: just as it is not accurate to label Europe and the United States as the Christian world and assume the European and US political world is normally determined by political Christianity, it is not accurate to assume that political Islam (or Islamism) is the general or the normal political outlook in the MENA region.

Eventually, the Israeli occupation will end, but the Palestinians will have the problem of Islamism to deal with. The former Palestinian ambassador to India, Osama Al-Ali, in a TV interview insisted that after the war the Gazans would kill every Hamas member they could find (Al-Ali 2024). Like everywhere else, the Islamists will not disappear without more bloodshed. Anywhere Islamism rose to power, it did so in the name of resistance of either foreign occupation or national dictatorship. However, there is not a case where the rise of Islamism has not become a bigger problem for the local population. The recent political history of Iran (1979–present), Sudan (1983–present), Afghanistan (1987–present), Iraq (2004–present), parts of Syria (2012–present), and parts of Yemen (2014–present) are among the examples. Given the ongoing presence of Islamism in the conflicts across MENA, we will continue to revisit the circumstances and consequences of its rise especially because relevant to its devastating influence on MENA societies there is not enough critical research about it in English, Arabic, Persian, or Turkish. Since the subject of this book is exclusionism in MENA, the problem of Islamism shall be analyzed in terms of geopolitics (e.g., the role of Iran, Turkey, and Qatar in Chapter 2), social movements (e.g., Sunni and Shia ideologies in chapters 2 and 3). Chapter 4 looks at an inclusive and egalitarian model that has been materialized in the pluralist enterprise of Northeast Syria, or Rojava, as an excellent alternative to be expanded in the post-nationalist and post-Islamist future of the Middle East. The final chapter revisits the problems of fascist exclusionism and identitarianism, leaving the reader with a concrete and comprehensive account of the book's critical thesis.

Main Arguments

The demise of the internationalist and secular movement of Marxism was not a separate event from the rise of ultra-nationalism and Islamism. Following decades of brutal crusades against Communists from Egypt to Indonesia, nationalists and Islamists became the only main political players. In reaction to the corruption of the nationalists' rule across the MENA region, Islamists presented themselves as the only option for populations who had suffered decades of bad education, poverty, and political oppression. While Islamists are still relatively small in numbers, they have been successful in deploying populist means to gain more sympathizers while deploying terrorism against populations whom they stand little chance of winning over.

Globally, right-wing politics have been on the rise for decades, and that is already catastrophic. What makes things even worse is that right-wing politics, including fundamentalism, of antagonistic camps could unwittingly reproduce each other endlessly. Islamism has been on the rise, and the majority of people in MENA have been brutalized by that. But those who have suffered the most are populations who, historically and presently, have been stigmatized and brutalized on racist and religious bases. This is why the struggle of anti-fundamentalists and anti-nationalists, which includes Arabs, Jews, Turks, Persians, Kurds, Yezidis, Zaza, Armenians, Assyrians, and Darfuris, can and should be comprehended politically as a struggle for emancipation.

This book primarily focuses on the present murky moment by examining the main aspects of exclusionary politics in MENA and shedding light on some of the hopeful prospects of resistance movements. The following is a breakdown of the main arguments:

1 Extremism in MENA is a feature of right-wing politics that followed the demise of leftist movements. I refute the common culturalist and homogenizing assumptions by showing that across the MENA region the rise of exclusionary movements coincided with the violent suppression of leftist movements which made up some of the most popular political parties. I argue that A. the current political scene in MENA could have taken a very different shape; and B. democratic and egalitarian resistant movements have never ceased to exist in the region.

2 To appreciate current and future struggles against exclusionism, it is imperative to comprehend the nature and the scope of the current crisis of the rise of right-wing politics in MENA, so the book aims to do just that by conducting critical analyses of two largely dismissed problems: the fascist perpetuation of racist politics.
3 While exclusionary movements continue to show multiple symptoms of fascism, fascism as a phenomenon remains severely understudied. Therefore, among the main objectives of this book is to problematize fascism in the context of a critical examination of the current historical moment in MENA politics.
4 Finally, if we look closely and if we stop dismissing the margins, inclusive and democratic alternatives have already been created and defended by both men and women, Muslims and non-Muslims, from various ethnic and national backgrounds. Therefore, a different MENA is possible.

The collapse of the Soviet bloc was followed by three decades of a continual rise of right-wing politics bringing the age of the neoliberal world order to new crossroads. However, today not only is an internationalist movement completely absent in the political sphere, but even anti-war movements such as those the world witnessed from the 1960s until the American invasion of Iraq in 2003 have almost completely disappeared, not to mention the absence of anything even remotely resembling the internationalist socialist movements that created a distinct and clear platform for opposing imperialist wars including WWI and WWII (see Lenin 1965; Lenin 2005; Debs 1939; Trotsky 1939). WWI was opposed by socialists from the United States, under Debs's leadership, to the Bolsheviks in Russia and Ukraine under Lenin's leadership. WWII was similarly opposed by the internationalists including Trotskyists and anarchists who desperately tried to stop the growth of fascism in Italy, Germany, and Spain.

The MENA region is going through one of its worst historical moments. Forty-three years after the Islamist takeover of Iran, almost 20 years after the fall of the Saddam Hussein regime in Iraq, and 12 years after the beginning of the Arab Spring, from Iran to Yemen, and from Iraq to Libya, violence and poverty have become normalized aspects of daily life. By the 1990s, it was clear that nationalism in all its variations had failed miserably across the region, so Islamism in its Shia and Sunni versions surfaced pushing the general public sphere further to the right.

It is well known that in the 1980s for the first time, jihadism was transformed into an international movement mobilized logistically and financially by a broad anti-communist alliance that included Saudi Arabia, Pakistan, and the United States. Jihadis were funded, armed, and sent to Afghanistan for the sole purpose of bringing down the socialist government in that country. In fact, none of these main supporters of the mujahedeen made their affairs with fundamentalist groups a secret. Both American journalism and the American official records from the 1980s make the alliance explicitly clear. As we will see later, even before Islamism started to gain some popularity, around the mid-twentieth century, the British colonial authorities used Islamic religious authorities and Islam politically to demonize Bolsheviks in Egypt (and other colonies) at a time when the Egyptian Bolsheviks seemed to be as popular as Russian Bolsheviks were in Russia of 1917 (Laqueur 1956, 277). After the colonial era, within the MENA region, various strategic anti-communist alliances were shaped between ultranationalists and Western powers.

In Turkey, Iran, and the Arab world, the communist opposition has always endured. Even today, much of what defines the secular and progressive movements of resistance in the region can be recognized by the Marxist phraseology that is adopted in their political discourse. One of the main objectives of this book is to shed light on the challenges with which emancipatory movements in MENA are faced. That said, this book does not claim to present a full account of all the sociopolitical conflicts in the MENA region. Rather, it is an attempt to illuminate the nature of the main exclusionary ideologies and movements in the region. Comprehending the ideological topography in terms of right versus left is essential for moving beyond the problematic, culturalist, assumptions about politics and social movements in the MENA region. If I ever get an opportunity to author another book on MENA, I will focus on the leftist struggles and the critique of the political economy and historical circumstances that conditioned the present gloomy moment.

The following five points clarify my overall position on MENA affairs:

1 Rejecting the common culturalist assumption by arguing that the problem is political, not cultural;
2 Rejecting the common idealist assumption: like all societies, the MENA societies are shaped by actual relations of domination between actual people as opposed to metaphysical beliefs and value systems;
3 Rejecting the orientalist assumption about Asian and African societies: at some point in recent history, egalitarian and emancipatory movements were the most popular movements across most

parts of Asia and Africa, and the struggle for equality and freedom may be weakened but has never been uprooted;

4 Asserting the basic historical truth of the political struggle for a universalist and inclusive transformation; and
5 Asserting that critically examining the scope of the crises and the magnitude of the hopelessness is essential for a historical transformation of the current moment.

Continuing the discussion initiated in this chapter, the second chapter provides a more in-depth analysis of the imperialist role the Iranian regime and the Turkish regime are playing in the Arab world and beyond using Islamism. While the book focuses on the rise of totalitarian, authoritarian, and fascist movements in MENA, the second chapter contextualizes the problem historically and presently. Even though I touch upon a few issues directly related to the Palestinian, Kurdish, Armenian, and Darfuri plights, I must state in clear words that this book falls short of presenting a comprehensive account of any aspect of any of those plights and their respective liberation movements. It is important to keep in mind that this book does not follow the traditional models in IR, whereby nation-states are the main units of study. Rather it is meant to offer a thematic and critical analysis of exclusionism in MENA while at the same time pointing to a glimpse of hope produced within the social movements in the region.

The third chapter is a critical examination of fascism within various right-wing movements in the Middle East. Fascism is one of the least studied questions in the Middle East, so problematizing it is essential to this book. There are many reasons for this gap in both fascism studies and Middle East studies. I think in fascism studies there is a common implicit premise that assumes that fascism as a phenomenon is unique to Europe. Superficially, this might sound politically correct, but upon a closer examination, it turns out that the assumption is deeply rooted in the typical set of orientalist beliefs according to which only Europeans could have a superiority myth, i.e., the non-European cannot even be fascist for fascism entails a degree of ideological sophistication and a sense of racial superiority. Also, as usual, non-European societies are more often than not assumed to be homogeneous, culturally predetermined, and ahistorical. It should go without saying that all societies have right and left-wing politics, and the myth of racial superiority, unfortunately, is not unique to European racism. If anything, while fascism in Europe obtained new masks and developed oblique discursive strategies of camouflaging in order to persist in the post-WWII era of liberal democracy, in MENA fascism has not been compelled to change its old, that is explicit, discourse. To appreciate the struggle of emancipatory movements and make progress toward recognizing the plight of the oppressed majority in MENA, it is imperative to make the critique of fascism a major debate in the public sphere.

Motivated by a critical epistemology, the method I deploy could be described as critical analysis of dominant frames of reference. Because similar subject matters are often lost between sociological versus metaphysical approaches, I intend to pay equal attention to both sides of the dualism. In the name of the multiplicity of interpretations the sociology of metaphysics has been undermined and religious texts and practices are usually exempted from critique and, thus, further metaphysicalized only using liberal/secular means. Therefore, I focus on critically analyzing Islamism's own justifications for committing social exclusionism and exclusionary politics of spatial production.

To present an existing alternative that has been invented and concretized in the region, the fourth chapter shifts the focus to a spot of hope, a margin where the horizon of possibility is broad and bright. In Rojava, which has been widely ignored by most scholars, something other than military rule and Islamism emerged. Rojava shows a multitude of unprecedented signs of a social revolution aimed at realizing inclusivity and egalitarianism. From my perspective, it makes sense that the left within such a stateless and doubly marginalized people, Syrian Kurds, would invent one of the most revolutionary formulae of social movements in the Middle East and the world (Ahmed 2022a).[4] The latest uprising in Iran that started in October 2022 after the murder of Mehsa Jina Amini on the hands of the regime's Morality Police in Tehran, a movement that spontaneously adopted the Rojava-Bakur resistance movement's motto *Jin, Jiyan, Azadi* (Ahmed 2022b), is indicative of the emergence of a new horizon of possibility from the margins of the margins (Ahmed 2022a; 2023a).

Chapter 5 returns to the broader view of the MENA region to articulate the critical philosophy of the book and the new ideas it offers. I argue that the Arab Spring's failure to bring about a more emancipatory situation is mainly due to the same issue that resulted in the rise of exclusionary, authoritarian, and totalitarian regimes. Namely, in the absence of an egalitarian revolutionary movement with a robust materialist account of history and social relations of power, and in the absence of a populace mobilized around a revolutionary doctrine of universal equality, the Arab Spring was doomed from the beginning, as was anticipated even at its start (Ahmed 2011). When the Arab Spring started, the Marxist left had already been weakened for decades. A large proportion of the youth who led the social movement, mobilized the public, and organized the protests did not have sufficient ideological resources to enable them in terms of a radical negation of the existing order. At best, they could have been described as liberals, elusively inspired by the attractive image of "democracy" Western liberal democracies had been marketing. However, liberalism has ceased to be a revolutionary ideology at least since the mid-nineteenth century. Even then, in its philosophical golden age, it was barely capable of exceeding the limits of bourgeois freedoms. That is to say, it simply lacked, and continues to lack, a doctrine of social justice beyond certain institutional and constitutional reforms. In the age of neoliberalism, the ideology has become far more reductionist no longer hiding its allegiance to the totalitarian rule of the market. What has remained of the attractions of liberalism, therefore, is a few fragmented and basic political performances such as free elections of legislative representatives and free speech, albeit, "free" in both cases are preconceived according to the bourgeois frame of reference, in which the absolutist rule of the market is both sanctioned and naturalized.

Free elections do not revolutionize any society that has suffered ages of exploitation and suppression. In most of the MENA region, in both so-called republics and monarchies, the (modern) state has never been fully born as the umbrella institution of the legislative, administrative, and public institutions. In my view, that is so, at least partly, because the (modern) state was not the result of social revolutions; rather, it was an immediate product of European colonialism. Also, more importantly, because the anti-colonial liberation movements were quickly halted after the "false independence" of these states in the region, we could see why "the state" is not what it is in the West. Put simply, the government is the state, and the state is the government in much of the MENA region. Therefore, bringing down a government often translates into bringing down the state, which is, needless to say, a disaster.

The Arab Spring's signature slogan, "the people want the dissolution of the regime," unsurprisingly, entailed a disaster. In most cases, Sudan being the most recent one, the fall of the regime amounted to the partial or complete fall of the state. In fact, when the Arab Spring took place, Iraq had already been living proof of the indistinguishability of the state and the ruling regime. While many millions of Iraqis had desperately dreamt of the day when the Baathist regime would fall, after 2003, the dream became a real nightmare when Iraqis from all backgrounds found themselves in a living hell due to the fall of the Baathist regime and, thus, the state as such. In fact, the Iraq case foreshadowed the failure of the Arab Spring. As it turns out, in most cases, with or without foreign occupation, a state's fate seems to be dependent on the fate of its ruling regime. What seems to make this hypothesis especially plausible in the case of the Arab majority countries is the historical fact that, unlike Persians and Turks who transited from empires to nation-states in the twentieth century, for most of the eight centuries preceding the rise of the Arab nation-states following WWI and WWII, with the a few short-lived and challenged exceptions, Arabs had not had sovereignty.

Sure enough, as soon as Arab regimes started to collapse during the Arab Spring, the Iranian and Turkish governments became the main two geopolitical players across the region from Iraq to Libya. Of course, the ruling regimes in Saudi Arabia, the UAE, and Qatar also played effective roles in the events across the Arab majority region, but they have never managed to formulate anything close to a political platform or a set of strategies representing a distinct front in International Relations. While Saudi Arabia drastically shifted its strategy since the beginning of King Salman's reign, opposing both the Sunni and Shia Islamist fronts, Qatar has continued a steady position of supporting Islamism in the Arab world and maintaining close relations with the Turkish and Iranian regimes. The UAE, Salman's Saudi Arabia, and El-Sisi's Egypt have been trying to form an Arab alliance against the increasing hegemony of Turkish (and Islamist) politics in the Arab world, but even this alliance has not been able to accomplish much in terms of the appeal to the broader Arab street. Ultimately, the Iranian regime has used Shia Islamism in its neo-imperialist enterprise, and the Turkish regime has utilized Sunni Islamism for its neo-imperialist expansion. Meanwhile, Arab geopolitical interests have been on a decline. Today, the Iranian regime has the final say in most of the decisive centers of power in Iraq, a significant influence in both Syria and Lebanon, and a primary role in the Houthi-controlled Yemen. The Turkish state has explicitly occupied parts of Syria and Iraq, and maintains a major role in the Libyan civil war as well rivalling the role of all the Arab states including Egypt.

During the Arab Spring, almost in every so-called "republic" in the Arab World, a naïve liberal elite agitated millions to bring down the state without daring, or even wanting, to touch the structures of social inequality. In fact, in most cases, just as the state was destroyed, the brutal state tools, such as the army, were both literally and figuratively embraced. If nothing else, the movement should have been on the reverse line of motion because that would have been more effective and reasonable. It is as if the formula for change was placed on its head from the beginning. Not surprisingly, the disillusioned majority found itself caught up in a Hobbesian nightmare of war of all against all. In every single case, from Tunisia to Syria, with the exception of a few margins explained in the second half of this book, people found themselves caught up in the worst possible dichotomy: the rule of generals versus the rule of Islamists.

Once more, the liberal promise of (bourgeois) democracy as the ultimate guarantor of political freedom and the neoliberal promise of the free market as the ultimate realization of a free society led to little more than the catastrophic collapse of the state (and its public institutions), blackmailing entire societies by their most pathological, exclusionary, and violent elements. The horrors that have taken place in Libya, Syria, and Yemen made the old times of dictatorship seem like a golden time in more than one sense, e.g., security, public health, education, rule of law, and the right to food and shelter. The Iranian and Turkish regimes and the Wahabis of the Gulf exploited the situation to the maximum degree to boost their respective hegemony in the region. Therefore, one of the main focuses of this book is the imperialist politics of Turkey, as today's main imperial camp of Sunni Islamism and Pan-Turkish nationalism, and Iran, as the world center of Shia Islamism and Islamist expansionism.

Notes

1 I am using the terminology as conceptualized and defined by Anibal Quijano (2000).

2 I have been writing about this since 2016 (e.g., Ahmed 2016a; 2016b; 2016c; 2016d; 2019a).

3 On February 2024, Human Rights Watch published a detailed report documenting wide human rights abuses targeting Kurds in the areas occupied by Turkish forces and the Islamist militia in Northern Syria (HRW 2024; also, for a report on the Turkish attacks between October 5–10, 2023, see HRW 2023).

4 This is also in keeping with Kathleen Arnold's thesis regarding political homelessness and cosmopolitanism (2004, chapter 5).

2 Islamism and the Geopolitical and Ideological Situation

Keeping the problem of identitarianism, especially culturalism, in mind, it is time to move to a direct analysis of the political circumstances in MENA, where Islamism is most aggressively represented by two imperialist camps: a Sunni front led by the Turkish state under Erdogan's party, and a Shia bloc led by the Islamic Republic of Iran. The former has found support among Islamist movements in Egypt, Libya, and Syria and the latter has seized many opportunities to expand its influence in Iraq (following the fall of Saddam Hussein's regime after the American invasion in 2003), in Yemen (with the Houthi takeover of the country in 2015 following the fall of Ali Abdullah Saleh's regime), and to some degree in Syria in the ongoing civil war.

The Demise of Progressive Movements and the Rise of the Right

It is not surprising that in the absence of a popular leftist movement the Arab Spring was swiftly hijacked by Islamist organizations. Nor is the return of one-man's rule in Egypt and Tunisia (and perhaps Libya as well) so surprising given the Islamist nightmare free elections could bring about for North African societies. A decade after the beginning of the Arab Spring, the threat of Islamism has proven that what is missing in the MENA countries is much more than free and fair elections. Today, it seems, for most Iraqis, Libyans, and Yemenis a return to one man's rule would be by far more favorable to any Islamist regime, which shows how tragically the Arab Spring has failed. It goes to show us how gloomy the current historical moment is, both socially and politically. Nonetheless, all hope is not lost. Also, as Chapter Five shows, there are innovative revolutionary movements in the peripheries of MENA that continue to resist the rule of both generals and imams, aiming to create inclusive social spaces and broad horizons of political possibility.

DOI: 10.4324/9781003351429-2

Across the Middle East and North Africa, up until the 1940s, socialist and communist movements were much more popular than both ultranationalist and fundamentalist forces. In fact, until the end of the 1960s, one could have hardly imagined that the right-wing would have any real prospect of becoming dominant for decades to come. Anywhere from Sudan and Yemen to Iraq and Iran, even in the Kurdish and Palestinian movements, the mainstream political discourses were produced by leftists and most of the phraseology was unmistakably and unapologetically Marxist. The fall into nationalist and sectarian politics paired with the decline of internationalist leftism reversed the prospects of emancipation across the region.

This leftist decline, in which Western powers also played a role by deploying all sorts of war strategies and culture industries, led to the rise of a number of exclusionary movements. Right-wing generals quickly took over most of MENA's newly established nation-states in the 1960s, 1970s, and 1980s. Also, in the absence of a popular left since the 1980s, religious fundamentalism, another representative of the far right, presented itself as the only alternative to the rule of generals from Algeria, Tunisa, Libya, Egypt, and Sudan to Syria, Iraq, and Yemen. Given these facts, the Arab Spring was in some ways bound to fail. Indeed, almost in every case, the uprisings were quickly highjacked by the fundamentalists who represented the most organized camp across the Arab World.

One of Walter Benjamin's profound observations is his assertion that behind every rise of fascism there is a failed progressive revolution (Žižek 2008, 386).[1] West Asia and North Africa were not exceptions in this regard. The communists had a significant role in leading the anti-colonial struggles especially in Egypt, Sudan, Yemen, Palestine, Lebanon, Syria, and Iraq. In fact, relative to the size of the respective populations, the number of revolutionary communists in some Middle Eastern countries was substantially larger than the number of Bolsheviks in Russia on the eve of the October Revolution (Laqueur 1956, 277).[2] Until the 1960s, it would have been hard to imagine that the right-wing would be able to defeat the left given the latter's ideological hegemony and wide popular support, especially among the emerging, yet influential, working-class across the region.

The British colonial administration felt threatened by a rising Bolshevik movement as early as 1919, and indeed the British administration enticed religious figures to issue anti-Bolshevik fatwas in an attempt to galvanize popular religious opposition against the Egyptian communists. On August 18, 1919, Muhammad Bakhit, the Grand Mufti of Egypt, the highest religious authority for issuing religious decrees, who was also rector of al-Azhar, issued a fatwa condemning Bolshevism as a threat to Islam and other monotheistic religions (Yaseen 2011, 17). The British colonial authorities widely distributed the fatwa in the colonies where Sunni Muslims were a majority. In the meantime, some other Islamic authorities had a different opinion in terms of the best way to prevent the appeal of Bolshevik communism; they claimed that the Quran had already guaranteed all the equalities the Bolsheviks call for (Yaseen 2011, 17).

In Palestine and Lebanon, there was a similar rise of working-class politics, and most of the communist leaders and intellectuals worked clandestinely to avoid arrest by the colonial rulers. Kurds, Armenians, and Jews, like Arabs, had a strong presence in both the communist partisan leadership and the communist intelligentsia across the Middle East, including Palestine, Lebanon, Syria, and Iraq. In Iran and Turkey, Kurds have always played a key role in the Marxist movement. In Iraq, both Jews and Kurds along with Arabs had a pioneering role from the early years of the Iraqi Communist Party (ICP). So much so that even today the Islamists and Pan-Arabists use anti-Semitic rhetoric to demonize the ICP. The ICP has been by far the most inclusive political party in the history of all political parties in Iraq. Also, the ICP was by far the most popular political party until the Baathists banned all political parties (for more see Franzén 2011). According to some estimates, when the population of Iraq was about seven million, there were about one million Iraqi communists. During the first nine months of the Baasthists' rule in 1963, the nationalists killed over half a million people on suspicion of being communists and raped around 100,000 women and girls within the same anti-communist campaign (Al-Sawt Al-Shuia'ai 1964, 6).[3] The tragic defeat of the left in the MENA region was followed by the age of right-wing politics of nationalism and Islamism.

Both Islamism, including its nationalist versions, and nationalism, including its religious versions, are inherently exclusionary and colonialist. It is self-evident that when a religion, any religion, is used as a means or measurement for founding a political community, exclusionism is already a predetermined sociopolitical outcome. Islam and Christianity have proven to be especially effective as imperialist ideological means for othering and subjugation. These two religions universal claims, which are rooted in their respective metaphysics, rendered them inherently expansionist and colonialist. There is barely any need to list historical cases to prove this. Those in the religious camps and their apologists, including some postcolonial scholars, would be quick to point to the cases in which Islamic and Christian communities have been oppressed and/or cases in which Islam or

Christianity have been used for anti-colonial ends. Of course, there is a lengthy list of such examples, but this assertion does not refute the main proposition with respect of the two religions' universal tendency for expansionism, domination, exclusionism, and, thus, colonialism.

Those perceived as Shia historically have been and in some places are still brutally oppressed. Indeed, Shia Islamism is founded on that deep sense of persecution and the desire for liberation. The grievances of Sunni Islamism mostly have to do with European colonialism and American imperialism. However, the legitimacy of the grievances does not make Islam as an institution and Islamism as an ideology emancipatory and egalitarian. Of course, there are many communities and persons in various parts of the world who face persecution because of their perceived or proclaimed Muslim identities. It is also true that Islam in multiple cases has been used to fight back against such oppressive systems and regimes. However, when it gains enough political and physical power, it behaves as a colonialist ideology without much consideration for the sufferings of the subjugated. In short, Islam is not inherently emancipatory,[4] and Islamism is inherently oppressive and colonialist.

If the era that followed European colonialism proved one thing, it is that nationalism and Islamism are themselves oppressive and colonialist forces. They may empower a group but only at the expense of other groups' lives, privileges, and freedoms. Therefore, the question of emancipation and decolonization is as relevant as it was a century ago when the Ottoman hegemony withered away and was replaced by European control. Also, as Engels emphasizes, a group of people that oppresses another group of people cannot be free (Engels 1874). Indeed, resistance movements that did away with nationalism have attracted members of privileged groups. For instance, the post-national Kurdish liberation movement is becoming increasingly popular among leftist Turks. The Rojava movement has attracted Arabs, Assyrians, Turks, and others into the project that is otherwise identified as a Kurdish movement. The same thing was true for the communist parties from Egypt and Sudan to Iraq and Iran. In their political platforms, these parties may have used the dominant language, e.g., Arabic or Persian; nonetheless, they attracted people from all linguistic and religious backgrounds, precisely because some of those who have been historically marginalized found hope for emancipation and egalitarianism in these parties.

In Egypt Nasserism and in Syria and Iraq Baathism were legitimized in the name of Arab sovereignty, anti-colonialism, and anti-imperialism. In each case, the moment the nationalists took over, they banned all political parties and criminalized democratic activities. Libya, Yemen, Algeria, Tunisia, and Sudan followed the same formula, which only ironically could be called "republican" because it is an extremely illiberal formula that barely recognizes any citizenry rights let alone political privileges that are supposed to be inherent in the very notion of sovereignty, according to republicanism, which emerged in modernity within the Enlightenment project. These brutal regimes in the cases of Tunisia, Algeria, Libya, Egypt, Yemen, and Iraq wiped out all the communist opposition. In Syria, the Syrian Communist Party was contained by the Baathist regime as one of the components of the national alliance led by the Baath Party, but all other Syrian communist groups were brutally suppressed. Across MENA, parallel to the decline of communism, there has been a proliferation of Islamism. In some cases, such as Anwar Sadat's regime, the government would allow a degree of Islamification and even tolerate some Islamist activities to eradicate the threat of communism. Generally, pointing to these regimes' corruption, political suppression of people, and alleged collaboration with Zionism, the Islamists presented themselves as the only viable alternative. Ironically, in Egypt, Sadat was assassinated by Islamists. The Shah of Iran had committed the same mistake of allowing the growth of Islamism to fight communism; sure enough, wherever they could, the Islamists wiped out the communists and quickly highjacked the Iranian revolution of 1979. The Islamist highjack of the 1979 revolution brought about the worst times for not only Iranians but also other peoples in the region who have been brutalized by Iranian-backed Islamist militia whether in Palestine, Lebanon, Yemen, Syria, or Iraq. The Islamist highjack of the Iranian Revolution foreshadowed the fate of the Arab Spring. In the Arab Spring too, Islamists swiftly exploited the state of unrest to become the primary alternative force, only this time around their prime partners to be pushed aside were liberals who other than the demand for regime-change, freedom of expression, and free and fair elections did not have much of a revolutionary platform. In Tunisia and Egypt, elections were perfectly suitable for the Islamists to come to power. In both cases, after a relatively brief period of Islamist rule, the one-man rule was brought back, creating a situation similar to the pre-Arab Spring. In Iran, however, the rule of Islamism persisted leaving many Iranians feeling nostalgic for the Shah era. In Syria, the same Islamist militia the Syrian regime supported to destabilize Iraq after 2003 started mobilizing against the Syrian state from 2011 onward. Across the region, Shia Islamism is backed by the Iranian regime, and Sunni Islamism by Erdogan's Turkey and Qatar.

Erdogan's Caliphate Project, the Islamist Reconquista, and Hamas

The world has been pushed into conflicts with endless global implications, and Erdogan's Turkey has been exploiting every possible regional and international conflict in a campaign to establish an empire that is no less devastating than the Third Reich. Unlike Hitler, however, Erdogan pragmatically combines both nationalist and religious means of populism to appeal to a much larger population of potential recruits across the world while succeeding to enjoy the ongoing support of opposed political forces from widely divergent sides of the ideological spectrum: Putin's Russia and the Western alliance; Turkish ultranationalists and Turkish Islamists; and frustrated Arab nationalists and Sunni Arab Islamists.

Acting as both a reincarnated Ataturk and Sultan, as both the Turkish nationalist father figure and the caliph of a multinational empire, Erdogan has been planning to celebrate 2023 for at least a decade, since the early days of the Syrian civil war, when he began sponsoring a seemingly endless number of Islamist groups. These twenty-first century janissaries, who often change their names and uniforms to take up whatever role may be assigned to them, are made up of Sunni Islamist fighters who have come from all parts of the world, including China, Central Asia, the Caucasus, North Africa, Europe, and the United States to fight under the banner of Ahrar al-Sham, Jaysh al Islam, Sultan Murad Brigade, Jund Al-Sham, al-Nusra Front, the Army of the Islamic Caliphate, Sultan Abdulhamid Han Brigade, ISIS, and many others. Supported sometimes openly, other times clandestinely, these movements have shared a unified strategy, and that strategy was conceived in Ankara. ISIS was merely a farcical (but instrumental) experiment, a trial balloon and a tool to finish some dirty business for the far more serious caliphate that Erdogan has been planning to launch.

It is no secret that Hamas's most prominent leaders and strategists have been based in Turkey for years. Nor is it a secret that Hamas, together with its financial backer Qatar, has expressed its enthusiastic support for Turkey's *fanaticalization project in Syria and the region.* Like Qatar, Hamas has preserved its conventional alliances with the Iranian regime and the Lebanese Hezbollah, but, also like Qatar, it is committed to a deeper and a more strategic and ideological allegiance to Erdogan's Sunni Islamist camp. In Syria, Sunni Islamists support Turkey, whereas Shia Islamists, including Hezbollah, are part of the Iranian proxies that support the Syrian regime. When the Syrian civil war broke out, relations between Damascus and Hamas deteriorated because Hamas did not side with the Syrian regime, which in turn affected the Iran-Hamas relations.[5] Then, by supporting the Sunni camp in Syria, Hamas revealed its true allegiance and placed itself against the Shia camp while preserving its peculiar relations with both the Iranian regime and Hezbollah.

"The Jerusalem Flood," as Hamas and its sympathizers called it, was self-evident as an expedition to take over Jerusalem by deploying a shock and awe strategy to paralyze Israel's ability to respond militarily and at the same time trigger a large uprising along with a religiously inspired overwhelming wave of popular support from the region to rapidly alter everything. Had things gone as planned, Erdogan would have come into the picture as the resurrected Selim he had been eagerly personifying and patiently preparing to announce in October 2023. As both the sultan and the caliph, the alleged man of the people whose *Islamic Reconquista* would be defended by the alleged *umma* across continents. Islamism entails preparedness to sacrifice any number of lives for a sanctified end, and Hamas has always been ready to use Palestinians as a means for that end.

Admittedly my argument about Turkey's potential involvement is a speculative one, but if one considers Erdogan's mindset especially in terms of his roleplay as the reincarnation of Selim I,[6] much of what otherwise appear puzzling would fall in place. Selim started his expansionist campaigns in the South Caucasus and the coast of the Caspian Sea then turned southward toward Aleppo, Damascus, Jerusalem, Gaza, Cairo, and Mecca and Medina, thereby announcing himself as the Caliph of Muslims in 1517. The trajectory of the events suggest that Erdogan had something similar in mind. Perhaps he was hoping that by October 29, his janissaries would win Jerusalem, only this time, instead of going from Jerusalem to Gaza as Selim's army did, Hamas would start the Jerusalem expedition from Gaza. Keep in mind Erdogan has done everything to take over northern, and possibly the rest, of Syria, but the presence of the Americans, the Russians, and the Iranians repeatedly curtailed his ambitions. His *Islamic Reconquista* could have had a better chance if his Syria expedition had been more successful or if the Muslim Brotherhood rule of Egypt had survived. For years, Erdogan was not prepared to come to terms with the end of the Muslim Brotherhood's rule, from 2012 to 2013. With the loss of a strategic ally of both Turkey and Hamas, Erdogan tried to make up for the loss on the Israel-Palestine flank, by supporting Hamas. Since then, Erdogan has increasingly given Hamas a bigger role there, or so it seems, as all of Israel's other land borders (i.e., Syria, Lebanon, and Jordan) remained out of reach for the Sunni Islamist camp. Hamas too was at a critical point after having been left at the mercy of its Shia allies, Iran and Hezbollah.

As a Sunni Arab Islamist movement, Hamas would never fully trust Iranian Shia Islamists, or any Shia Islamist group, or any Shias tout court. The man who founded Hamas as the Muslim Brotherhood's offshoot in the Palestinian territories explained in very clear terms that their relations with the Iranian regime were purely defined by common interests. While Hamas uses the Iranian regime to receive weapons and funds, as a native Palestinian group, Hamas is considered a special asset for any Islamist camp, including the Shia camp.

In the Arab world, the Hamas leadership could justify their allegiance to Erdogan on a religious basis, but they could not do the same when it came to their relations with the Shia camp, a fact widely understood in the Arab world. Most in the region accept that the Hamas-Tehran link is a pragmatic relationship necessitated by circumstances. Hezbollah, on the other hand, is perceived as an Iranian proxy. Even if circumstances necessitate building good relations with Hezbollah, essentially, it is perceived with suspicion, as a force with Shia and Persian allegiances. The equivalent of the religiously cemented alliance between Tehran and Hezbollah is the alliance between Ankara and Sunni Islamist groups from Al-Nusra and ISIS to the Muslim Brotherhood and Hamas.

The evidence suggests that Hamas kept its plan for the October 7 attack secret from its Shia allies. In fact, it seems that Hamas's leadership took extraordinary measures to conceal their plan from their Iranian and Lebanese friends. American officials have repeatedly stated that they have not detected any signs indicating the *direct* involvement of the Iranian regime. Had the Iranian regime or Hezbollah been informed about the Hamas plan, presumably they would have taken steps to prepare for a potential war. Available information suggests that no such preparations had been made. As I anticipated during the early weeks of the war (Ahmed 2023c), the farthest the Iranian regime went in the conflict was to have Hezbollah distract part of the IDF forces on Israel's northern border and Shia militias threaten American forces in Iraq and Syria. In terms of its own military logistics inside Iran, the regime has been careful not to do anything that might suggest that it intends to get directly involved in the war. The Iranian officials use threatening language against Israel, but that is nothing out of ordinary from the perspective of the regime's political and ideological schizophrenia.

Anti-Israeli and anti-American rhetorics are something the regime will always deploy because that rhetoric has become part of its identity. More often than not, the regime does what it does not say. It does not say that it will enter the conflict directly on Hamas's behalf, and it will not. Meanwhile, it does what it strongly denies. For instance, it has been insisting that it is not interested in obtaining nuclear weapons, yet obtaining nuclear weapons is at the top of its priorities. Much of this double personality is rooted in the regime's fear of its own collapse. Such fears are somewhat normal for a totalitarian regime because those at the top of the police state distrust their people. What might make the case confusing, especially for those who are not familiar with the nature of the regime, is that it is not a typical totalitarian state. As a so-called "Islamic republic," its discourse reflects the schizophrenia of a retrogressive but modern entity that tries to be both a nation-state and an Islamic state at the same time. The regime's discourse is symptomatic of the rulers' fears and intentions but only in a roundabout and pathological way. There is a chasm between the official discourse and the state policy both internally and externally.

For most people in the Middle East, including and especially Iranians and Arabs, it is almost common knowledge that Khamenei will continue exploiting the Palestinian plight, but, at least intentionally, he will never turn the conflict with Israel or the United States into a full-blown war. Following the October 7th attack, one of the trending themes in Arabic on social media platforms was the mocking of the Iranian regime and its proxies in Iraq, Syria, and Lebanon about their empty threats against Israel. Yet, somehow, most Middle East specialists seem to have fallen for the Iranian regime's propaganda, which is comically bad anyway not despite but especially because of its militaristic and antagonistic language.

The rulers of Iran realize that direct external conflicts might weaken their hold on the means of terror against their own people, which could in turn encourage the people of Iran to seize the opportunity to bring down the regime. The regime's aggressive discourse of course has ramifications, but in terms of policy, the aggressions are conducted carefully and mainly through proxies. Only if and when a perceived enemy is too weak to strike back, will the regime implicate itself directly. As many in the Middle East would know as a matter of common sense, Khamenei will not risk his Shia state for the plight of Sunni Arabs in Gaza, some of whom, from his perspective, are still loyal to Saddam Hussein's legacy, the Iranian regime's most hated enemy.[7]

To Khamenei's bitter disappointment, no matter how hard he tries to appear loyal to the Palestinian issue, for the majority of conservative and non-conservative Sunnis, Khamenei remains a sectarian Iranian leader. He barely has any sympathizers outside Iran with the exception of a few conservative Shia outposts in other countries. Moreover, in Iran, his regime cannot survive without deploying constant means of terror, having become increasingly unpopular in recent years among all Iranian religious and ethnic groups, including the Shias, who have become increasingly distrustful of his regime and of the Shia militias. To say nothing of Iraqi Sunnis who see his regime as the main threat to them or Iraqi Kurds who normally identify with the Kurdish plight in Iran.

Like Khamenei, Erdogan often does what he does not say. However, unlike Khamenei, he rarely says or implies what he does not intend to do. The supreme leader of the Islamic Republic expresses his support for jihadism, especially in relation to Jerusalem as part of his routine rhetoric. In contrast, as the head of the supposedly secular Turkish state, Erdogan usually avoids expressing support for jihadism openly (which might have changed had the conflict opened up an opportunity for him to appear as the victorious sultan); instead, he supports jihadist campaigns, by calling them something else and amending the rhetoric according to circumstances. In short, for the most part, he does what he does not say. This is the reason for Erdogan's bifurcated behavior as the head of a double state: superficially staying within the secular parameters of a secular state while practically accelerating the full Islamification of politics. In other words, just as an essential part of Khamenei's job is to sound supportive of jihadism especially vis-à-vis the Islamic religious claim of Jerusalem, part of Erdogan's job is to sound secular and peaceful even when he supports Islamist movements that openly deploy terroristic means. But all that began to change about a decade ago. Erdogan's supporters had been assuring Islamist sympathizers that in the year 2023 they would all see the ultimate Islamic victory in the form of the revival of the Ottoman Caliphate.[8]

In 2013, Erdogan started to allude to reviving Ottoman hegemony as he also began orchestrating Turkish politics internally, regionally, and globally in accordance with that objective. While support for Khamenei's regime could not exceed Shia Islamist militias and some conservative Shias in Iran, Iraq, Yemen, and Lebanon, Erdogan has been enoying substantial support from an ever-growing base among conservative Sunnis in the region: among conservatives, Islamists, and nationalists within Turkey, among pan-Turkic nationalists in the Middle East and parts of Asia; and among most Islamist sympathizers and nationalists in the Arab world. His base seems to be growing in parts of North Africa and sub-Saharan Africa as well, for example, in Libya, Somalia, and Senegal. Erdogan has also been appealing to Pan-Turkic sentiments to gain support in Central Asia and the South Caucasus while putting more emphasize on Pan-Islamic rhetoric in the Balkans, Western Europe, and North America. Both regionally and globally, at times modestly, at other times extraordinarily, the support for Erdogan's brand of Islamist populism is far larger than anything Khamenei or any other Shia Islamist leader could ever have aspired to, in large part due to sectarian conflicts that have divided Islamic sects and institutions for centuries.

Erdogan, of course, avoids not only direct conflict but also antagonistic discourse against Israel and the West although in his public speeches often he sounds less friendly toward the West and Israel, which has to do with maintaining his populist image as the strong sultan and the would-be-caliph. Erdogan has a much stronger populist base across a wide number of nationalities, sects, and geographic areas because he can count on something Khamenei cannot, namely he can play the role of the present-day caliph, the leader of the so-called *umma*. On the other hand, and mainly because Shias are a minority among Muslims, a Shia leader will never be perceived as anything other than that, a Shia leader. Even though most Islamist leaders, including Khamenei, usually avoid references to the sectarian terminology and instead present themselves in terms of the unifying religion, the political status of a Shia leader is bound to be perceived in sectarian terms. To Erdogan, and other Sunni Islamists, a caliphate symbolizes imperial Islamic glories. To Khamenei, and his Shia sympathizers, the term "caliphate" invokes the greatest of all grievances – the ultimate tragedy of historical injustices and sufferings inflicted on the Shias, on those who stayed faithful to "Ahl al-Bait."[9] Of course, most of those who are perceived as Sunnis or Shias whether Iranians, Azerbaijanis, Central Asians, Turks, Arabs, Kurds, or Amazigh, do not support Islamism; otherwise, we would be living in a much gloomier world. Nonetheless, with the exception of Iran, there has been a rise of Islamism in MENA region. Given the extremist nature of Islamism as an ultraconservative and ultra-right movement, even a slight increase in the number of Islamist supporters and sympathizers should be cause for serious concern.

October 2023 was the centennial of the establishment of the Republic of Turkey, the founders of which were also the engineers of the Armenian and Dersim genocides. Among these founders was the godfather of Turkish nationalism, Mustafa Kemal Ataturk, who, as Stefan Ihring has shown, was Mussolini's and Hitler's most inspiring hero (Ihring 2014). Erdogan was hoping to celebrate Turkey's 100th anniversary, by creating a new empire, while both renewing the historic genocidal goals of Ataturk and expanding Islamism.[10] And with that goal in mind, Erdogan has been using Hamas to exploit the Palestinian question, turning its militia into his valued janissaries, who are serving his most sensitive Islamist mission outside Turkey (Ahmed 2016a; 2016b; 2016c; 2016d; 2019c). Behind Erdogan's popularity there are many reasons, but key to his success is his remarkable opportunism. As a populist leader he is always ready to strike against the least empowered political player in any crisis and at any critical turn of events. Needless to say, the MENA region has never failed to provide him with opportunities in the form of crises and what to most people would be disastrous turns of events.

Being the opportunistic populist demagogue he is, Erdogan does not miss a chance to use his enablers. Those enablers include Western leaders who never dared stand up to his politics of blackmailing; Putin who is prepared to do his bidding because he sees Erdogan as his best hope for keeping NATO from destroying holy Russia; and a sizable number of frustrated Arab opinion makers who, having lost faith in Arab nationalism, see Erdogan as a new father figure who has seemingly come to their rescue after a long era of defeat, following the failed wars with Israel in 1967 and 1973. Erdogan wants to keep Turkey's good relations with the West as much as possible while at the same time he works tirelessly to revive the Ottoman caliphate and become the sultan of the *umma*. The Turkish state is a peculiar case. It is neither a liberal democracy nor a totalitarian state. It is more like a double state.

Reportedly, Suleyman Demirel once said, "there are two states. There is the state and there is the deep state … When a small difficulty occurs, the civilian state steps back and the deep state becomes the generator" (qt. in Gunter 2014, 31). Demirel put it even more pointedly stating that "the deep state is the state itself. It is the military" (qt. in Kanli 2007).[11] Ironically, but not without a sense of cynicism, Kenan Evren who removed Demirel through a military coup to place himself as the president for seven years starting in 1982, confirmed Demirel's statement adding, "when the state is weakened, we take it over. We are the deep state" (qt. in Gunter 2014, 32). Even Erdogan admitted the existence of the deep state and alluded to its roots in the Ottoman Empire (Torchia 2007). The Turkish Republic is ultimately a two-layer state, an outer institutional and constitutional one and an inner undemocratic and clandestine one.

However, at least in terms of the 2013–2023 phase of Erdogan's reign, "deep state" is rather misleading. I think something like "the inner layer of the state," "the top state," or "the super-state" would be more accurate because we are in fact speaking of the most powerful center of decision making and clandestine executive networks that are not accountable to any of the constitutional and legal apparatuses of the state, let alone the public. As a matter of fact, all this is characteristic of dictatorships. In a dictatorship, the leader dictates decision making in the most sensitive realms including especially the securitization of the public sphere and the deliberate undemocratization of the political sphere. In the case of Erdogan's Turkey, in addition to those two characteristics, the imperialization of foreign policy is also taking place, rendering Erdogan more than just a sultan or a caliph. In fact, Erdogan is a textbook example of a fascist leader. All this is even more applicable in the case of the Islamic Republic of Iran, and its *Murshid* (the German word for *Murshid* is Führer).

For fascists, the state is a mere means for the resurrection of the glorious nation, and the state apparatuses are, therefore, useful only as far as they can be manipulated for the sake of reviving the alleged superiority of the alleged nation. From that perspective, the citizen belongs to the state, and the state belongs to the nation. The nation in the nationalist sense is something to be restored to its mythical glories. The nation in the sense of the people, the population within the boundaries of the state, are *ra'iyat*, a flock to be herded by the state and shepherded by the leader. While shepherding his subjects, the leader is determined to revive the assumed greatness of the assumed nation. The leader holds the image of the nation very close to his heart while he holds contempt for the *ra'iyat*. The leader can sacrifice any number of the members of his *ra'iyat* whenever and however he deems appropriate. The *ra'iyat* are the leader's stuff as opposed to autonomous subjects with intrinsic rights to life. To the fascist leader, the existing individual is nothing and the reascending nation is everything. Ironically, every fascist leader, if not stopped, will only succeed in destroying the state in every sense, universalizing violence in all directions, mass displacing entire populations, and totalizing destruction spatially.

Like Iranian officials, Turkish officials are regularly operating on two levels, one to deceive and another to accomplish their objectives. On the level of deep state, all measures are taken in order to leave no trace whatsoever of the state's extralegal activities. Iranian officials know that everyone knows that they are responsible for Hamas's acts. Turkish officials on the other hand know that if they leave no evidence, the chances are that they could not only get away with masterminding such incursions as the attack on Israel on October 7, but cause another international conflict as well, between various states in the region and the West, creating yet another golden opportunity for Turkey to benefit from these crises.

For ten years Erdogan had been planning to reveal himself as the hero of an Islamic Reconquista in the fall of 2023. Reinventing himself as the contemporary Sultan Selim I, Erdogan envisioned redrawing the political map of Eurasia and North Africa. Had Hamas succeeded in its "Jerusalem Flood" operation, Erdogan would have been able to mark October 2023 as the beginning of a new Ottoman era. Like Khamenei, but using a different strategy, Erdogan seems to be prepared to fight Israel to the last drop of Palestinian blood. Despite the differences between the Sunni and Shia Islamist camps in terms of tactics and discourses, Hamas plays the same role for both sides in the sense that it fully executes the principle of fighting the Israeli army to the last Palestinian civilian, and, conveniently for Hamas, most Palestinians have no access to any fortified underground tunnels to protect them from bombardment or the option of resigning to luxury resorts in Turkey and Qatar.

What did October 7 Reveal about Sunni and Shia Islamism?

To recapitulate, Hamas could never have organized such a sophisticated attack on Israel, consisting of so many different military technologies, precisely coordinated from air, land, and sea, without substantial prior training by military experts and long-term access to *open-air* army facilities. It is inconceivable, for example, that on its own Hamas could have trained so many paraglider users to navigate, maneuver, and shoot with such ease. Also, the manufacturing of the drones, the necessary training of drone operators, and the logistics needed for coordinating the rocket attacks would have been impossible without the kind of expertise, space, and resources that only a state could afford.[12]

In theory, the Syrian or the Iranian regime could have been the main sponsor of Hamas's attack. But the evidence points more likely to Turkey. There is no doubt that the Iranian regime funds and arms Hamas, and it is highly likely that Hamas have been using some of those arms, but, to reiterate, there is no evidence to date that the Iranian regime knew anything about the attack before the morning of October 7, when the attack was already underway. In my estimation, officials within the second layer of the Turkish state might have had prior knowledge about the attack.

In the case of the Iranian regime, as it capitalizes on anti-Israeli populist Islamism in the region, it regularly overstates its intentions to strike the Jewish state. At the same time, given how unpopular and fragile the regime is at home, when the Israeli army stroke back on Gaza, the Iranian mullahs could not risk engaging in a direct conflict with Israel and/or the United States. Instead, they simply talked tough, reproducing the regime's image as Israel's most dangerous enemy. Meanwhile, the Khamenei regime continued to use its proxies, like Hezbollah and the Houthis, to maintain a state of neither war nor peace.

Confirming Iran's reasons for remaining cautious, Israel had been keeping a close eye on its military activities, not only in Iran but also in Syria and elsewhere in the Middle East. Under these circumstances, it was unlikely that a campaign of the magnitude of the one Hamas launched on October 7, would have eluded the Israeli intelligence apparatus. In theory Syria too could have trained Hamas militants to launch this sophisticated attack but, given the destruction of the country over the last ten years of civil war and the regime's careful avoidance of provoking Israel, that possibility can be ruled out as well. The Israelis had been watching Assad and his allies very closely and had been systematically bombing Iranian and Hezbollah military facilities in Syria. Turkey, on the other hand, enjoyed the privileges of a Western ally whose Islamist activities were not scrutinized with the same degree of suspicion. The Turkish state has the technology, the expertise, and the logistics to train not hundreds or thousands but tens of thousands of jihadis to play their role in an imperial enterprise. Everything that happened since the rise of ISIS suggests that Turkey indeed has done exactly that.

Throughout the last decade, Erdogan has blackmailed Europe by using the refugee card. If the European Union wanted Erdogan to manage what has tastelessly been called the "refugee crisis," it would have to provide Turkey with billions of dollars to deal with the Syrian, Iraqi, and Afghan refugees seeking to settle in Europe. The EU would also have to refrain from criticizing Erdogan's regime for its continual violations of the EU regulations and international law. What is more, Turkey played a major role in creating the crisis in the first place by supporting the jihadi groups whose violence displaced millions of people. Erdogan used the same strategy with the crisis in Ukraine, turning it into an opportunity, by forcing NATO to acquiesce to Turkey's political demands. First, before Erdogan would lift his objection to the admission of Sweden and Finland into the alliance, the two countries had to agree to turn over to the Turkish government Kurdish refugees, who had fled Turkey and were now living within their borders, even though these Kurdish exiles supposedly enjoyed international protection. Second, Turkey insisted that the United States resume sales of F16 fighter jets to Turkey, which the US had halted after Turkey began purchasing Russian S-400 air-defense systems.

In Syria, as the Turkish-backed jihadis failed to take over the country, Erdogan entered into another opportunistic game with the most powerful parties on the Syrian stage, Putin's forces, the Iranian regime, and the Americans, to eliminate the Kurdish majority self-administrated Northeast Syria. For instance, Erdogan persuaded Putin to withdraw his so-called Russian peacekeepers from the Kurdish city of Afrin (Dirik 2018).[13] In doing so, he opened the way for the Turkish army and its Islamist proxy militias to shell the city and its surrounding areas heavily for weeks before taking control of the region entirely in March 2018.[14] Five years later, in 2023, in a similar move Erdogan persuaded Putin to restrain the Russian peacekeeping forces in Nagorno-Karabakh from doing anything to prevent the Azerbaijani takeover of land claimed by both Armenia and Azerbaijan, which resulted in another mass displacement of Armenians.

Today, the global capital of Sunni Islamism is Ankara, while the capital of Shia Islamism is Tehran. Sunni and Shia Islamists have constructed various secret organizations, propaganda apparatuses, and militant proxies to deploy different populist and terroristic means in different places. Erdogan made use of the notion of the "Islamic nation" to mobilize and recruit tens of thousands of refugees to join Islamist groups in Syria, Libya, and beyond. The Iranian regime's influence is focused on Shia populations and organizations in Iraq, Yemen, Syria, and Lebanon. While Hamas is a Sunni Islamist group, it is in the unique position of enjoying the support of both Ankara and Tehran. The reasons for this, while complex, are not unrelated to Hamas's stated goal of destroying the State of Israel.

Gazans and their plight have been exploited by Hamas and other Islamist groups, but Gaza is certainly not the headquarters of Islamism. Ankara and Tehran are. While the ruling regime in Tehran loudly expresses its support for Sunni Hamas in addition to Shia Hezbollah, most of what that regime expresses is little more than empty propaganda and false alarms. The regime's main concern is its own survival in Iran. Khamenei seems to believe, perhaps accurately, that any form of direct military conflict with Israel and/or the United States would result in the collapse of his regime. No doubt the Islamic Republic of Iran is the conventional patron of Hamas and Hezbollah, but Khamenei would not make such a suicidal move as the October 7th attack especially at a time when his regime is facing a popular revolution aimed to end the Islamic Republic. Erdogan, on the other hand, has been patiently building his Sunni Islamist empire, utilizing his relations with Islamist groups, pan-Turkic movements, Putin's regime, and NATO. As Turkey mobilizes Islamists across the Middle East and in the Caucasus, it will only create more chaos in an already disastrous world. Erdogan's caliphate will continue to give rise to Islamists everywhere, and brutalizing civilians in Gaza will only help provide more potential recruits for his janissaries.

There is no Such Thing as "Islamist Resistance"

Islamism is a death cult, and the cheapest thing in Islamists' world-view is human life. An Islamist group celebrates the death of the people it claims to defend and the death of those against whom it has announced a religious war. Islamists systematically capitalize on death. Among their perceived enemies, they try to kill as many people as possible, and they present this as heroism and acts of religious piety. Among their perceived "nation of Islam," they try to cause the death of as many people as possible, and they use this to claim collective victimhood thereby imposing themselves as the rightful avenge takers of the people they allegedly represent. All their inventions are focused on maximizing casualties. To Islamists, the highest merit is the production of death, as the means and the end.

Islamism has never liberated any group of people anywhere in the world.[15] A movement that openly devalues human lives cannot be liberating on any level. If a religious or nationalist movement exploits legitimate grievances of an oppressed people to justify its own existence, that only makes it more, not less, problematic. If an argument or a policy, whether knowingly or unknowingly, entails the Islamist premise of death, it will only help further human destruction and produce more fanatic forms of Islamism. Hamas, for instance, wants to dictate the fate of all Palestinians, who already live in a desperate and hopeless situation. And it is a catastrophic mistake for both supporters of Palestinian independence and the supporters of Israel to equate Hamas with the Palestinian people, including the residents of Gaza.

That said, it is simply false to claim that Hamas's acts are a reaction to Israeli politics against Palestinians or to claim that Islamism is not fundamentally anti-Semitic. Islamists have a pathological hatred for Jews and for the disempowered religious minorities. Conflating Islamist violence with anti-colonial resistance is deeply deceptive. Sometimes the false argument is made from a position of sympathy for the

Palestinian plight but it stems from sheer ignorance of what Islamism represents. The Islamists' propaganda wants everyone in the world to believe their movement is an anti-colonial and anti-imperial one, but Islamism itself is a colonialist and imperialist project in which every human life is a deadly means for a deadly end. In MENA, only Islamists, such as the Muslim Brotherhood and the Iranian regime, perceive Islamism as the natural political expression of Islam and the legitimate voice of Muslims. Most Muslims, like most non-Muslims, in the Middle East have been struggling against the rise of Islamism. In the West, those who perceive Islamism as the self-evident political expression of Muslims unknowingly adopt a racist mode of perception that is premised on the homogenization and culturalization of the MENA societies as societies primarily defined by religion and religious politics, unlike white-majority societies where various political movements from ultraright to radical left exist. In other words, from the racist point of view, it is not conceivable that in MENA societies too there is a spectrum of political movements from the far right, such as Islamism and ultranationalism, to the far left, such as communism, with a majority being near the center.

In conclusion, clarifying the basic premises of Islamism is in order. Islamism has treated people everywhere, including those who, like Palestinians, are stateless with similar hatred, brutality, and total disregard for anything remotely relevant to social and political emancipation. Yezidis in Sinjar or Afrin did not have any conflicts whatsoever with Muslims or Arabs anywhere, but they have been subjected to the same kind of jihad and worse. Kurds in Rojava are stateless and have already been brutalized continually for the last one hundred years, but they are subjected to sheer terror every day by Syrian, Turkish, and other Islamists. Islamism has been treating the Fur and other black Africans in Sudan with the same barbarism and worse. Buying into the Islamist discourse imposed by Hamas about Palestinians is especially unfair for the Palestinians even if a relatively large number of them, out of sheer frustration, have become Hamas sympathizers. Those who are trapped in Gaza between the worst of all possible options. Many of them were born into a world of violence and humiliation. For those of us who are not trapped in such a world, there is no excuse not to see that the Palestinian plight and Hamas are two different things. Neither the Palestinian plight should be criminalized because of Hamas, nor Hamas should be justified in the name of the Palestinian plight.

Often the traditional left in the West and Latin America conflate Islamist movements in the Middle East such as Hamas and Hezbollah with leftism. While Middle Eastern politics and ideological topographies are extremely complicated and problematic, nobody in the region would confuse Islamism with leftism. In certain contexts of nationalism and national liberation movements, right versus left distinctions could become blurry, but the designation of Islamism as an ultra-right-wing movement, fundamentalism, and ultra-conservatism is self-evident. Meanwhile, associating Islamism with normative Middle Eastern politics is rooted in an orientalist, or, more accurately, culturalist, perception that presupposes homogeneity and essentialism about the peoples of MENA. It is ironic when anti-colonialist, post-colonialist, liberal, and progressive academics and thinkers unwittingly adopt and reproduce such a perception. Their friendly intentions toward the peoples of the region only make their implicit culturalism intellectually and politically more absurd.

Finally, Islamism is first and foremost a problem for the people in the region. Eventually there must be a process of de-Islamification of politics led by Arabs, Turks, Persians, Kurds, Azeris, Baluchis, Punjabis, Pashtuns, Amazigh, etc. The Kurdish led left-wing movement in Turkey and Syria and many Iranians from various parts of Iran have already established popular fronts against Islamism. As Chapter 5 of this book argues, the intelligentsia in MENA and beyond would do well if they turn to these movements for both solidarity and inspiration. After all, as an imperialist project, Islamism wants to take societies centuries back to the rule of bashas and imams. If they are not stopped, nobody in MENA will be saved from their subjugation.

Of course, Islamism is not the only major crisis in MENA. Nor is it true to assume that Islamism is separate from nationalism and its crises. To make the critique of exclusionary politics in MENA more comprehensive, the next chapter turns to the problem of fascism in MENA. The fact that fascism has scarcely been problematized in MENA is enough reason to make us concerned about every aspect of knowledge production and politics regardless of whether labeling some fundamentalist and ultranationalist movements as fascist is deemed justifiable or not. The problematization of fascism as "a form of ideology" ensures keeping our critical and analytic doors open for applying ideology critique across all borders and boundaries, discourses and disciplines, and so on.

Notes

1 This is based on Žižek's wording of an idea induced from what Benjamin expressed loosely with regard to the rise of fascism following WWII, so

Žižek himself deserves equal credit for the statement, "behind every fascism there is a failed revolution" (quoted in Žižek 2008, 386).

2 Walter Laqueur may be right that nationalism arrived in the Middle East without its liberalizing and democratic objectives, but his portral of European nationalism as a successful model, if anything, is indicative of his own biases. Those biases become too clear from the first few pages of the book as he insists on grouping communism, in the Middle East and everywhere else, as inherently illiberal and anti-democratic, just like Islamism and nationalist chauvinism (Laqueur 1956, 7–9).

3 As the editors of this source state, the book is a collection of historical documents that had been issued by the nationalists. The editors, therefore, emphasize that any accusation of the communists of fabricating numbers and events or committing exaggeration in the estimated numbers of victims would be irrelevant (Al-Sawt Al-Shuia'ai 1964, 7).

4 For centuries, Islam, as a social and political institution, was the main justifier of the enslavement of Africans, and enslavement was a main tool for spreading Islam in Africa (for more, see, for instance, Hardy 2002).

5 Khalid Mashaal in an interview admitted that their relations with Iran were affected after Hamas refused to take the Syrian regime's side in the civil war (Aljazeera 2016). More recently, Mashaal admitted that over the years Iran supplied them with weapons and funded them, but in the same interview he also sent a veiled complaint to the Iranian regime and Hezbollah about not doing more after the October 7 attacks (Al-Arabiya 2023). This was interpreted as implying that Iran and Hezbollah betrayed Hamas at the most decisive moment, following the October 7th attack.

6 For a brief overview of Erdogan's identification with Salim I, see the section titled, "CODA: Shadows over Turkey" in Alan Mikhail's *God's Shadow: The Ottoman Sultan Who Shaped the Modern World* (Mikhail 2021). I think the book commits a degree of romanticization of the Ottoman Empire to counteract works that vilified Muslims for a long time, but the work is nonetheless praiseworthy for its large scope yet good focus and for its writing style.

7 While Khamenei speaks in the name of the "Islamic world," he knows that in reality neither Sunni Islamists nor Arab nationalists would ever see him as anything but an enemy. The distrust between Sunnis and Shias has a long history starting in the seventh century and continuing into the Safavid-Ottoman conflict in the sixteenth century and later. The same antagonism erupted again in the form of the Iraq-Iran war of the 1980s, and the civil war in Iraq in the twenty-first century.

8 At least in 2014–2015, when I was in Turkey, this element of ideological mobilization was so prevalent, that one could sometimes overhear it being mentioned in public spaces in certain conservative demographics. For more on my observations about this over the years, see Ahmed 2016a; 2016b; 2016c; 2016d; 2019c.

9 The literal meaning of Ahl Al-Bait is *people of the house* (of Mohammed). For Shias, it refers to Fatima, Ali, Hassan, and Hussein.

10 It is probable that the selection of the date also had something to do with Erdogan's obsession with Selim I, who was born on October 10, 1470. Erdogan's hero is Sultan Selim I, the first Ottoman caliph who ruled over Islam's holy cities. During his reign, 1512–1520, the Ottomans took over

Palestine along with Egypt, Syria, and Hijaz, stretching the empire from the Azov Sea and the Black Sea to the Mediterranean Sea and the Red Sea, from Crimea to Greece and from Bosnia and Moldova to southern Hijaz and Egypt.

11 For more on the deep state and Demiral's comment, also see Giragosian 2007, 38; Filiu 2015, chapter 1; Gunter 2014; Torchia 2007; Şen 2021.

12 Even the official Turkish state television broadcast a detailed report about the Turkish secret police's protection of one of the masterminds behind the cyber-attack on Israeli military facilities (TRT 2023).

13 Putin's withdrawal of his peacekeepers foreshadowed his betrayal of the Armenians of Nagorno-Karabakh where Russian peacekeepers had been stationed.

14 The city and its surrounding areas have been almost emptied of its Kurdish inhabitants and replaced by Arab Islamist settlers and their families (Kajjo 2019).

15 Furthermore, historically, Islam has been an imperial religion since its early days, that is, when the founder of the *ummah*, Muhammed, was still alive (e.g. see Al-Qumni 1996; Karsh 2013).

3 The Fascist Aspects of Exclusionism in the Middle East

It is time to turn to the problem of fascism in the Middle East discussing the need for problematizing fascism in the Middle Eastern public sphere. After looking into the history of several waves of nationalism and their affinity with Italian and German fascism, we may be able to better appreciate the challenges with which resistance movements are faced. We need to learn about the history and the persisting threat of fascism in Turkey, Iran, and the Arab world. While a comprehensive study of fascism in MENA may not be feasible within the limited space of this book, an overview of the fascist affinities of nationalist ideologies, movements, and regimes in the era that followed the demise of communism is in order. I treat "fascism" as a form of ideology, not in the historically and geographically limited sense. There are some important scholarly works that address the phenomenon of fascism in Turkey and the Arab World, but within fascism studies overall, the area remains extremely under-studied. In the absence of such debates, the marginalized majority have been brutalized in the region for decades, and some of the most creative movements of resistance have been ignored by the intelligentsia.

The Fascist Moment in Dialectics of Enlightenment

To problematize the politics of exclusion in MENA, the nationalist bourgeoisie and fundamentalist religious ideologues should be *historically* held accountable, not the majority of ordinary Turks, Arabs, Persians, Kurds, Turkmens, etc., even if and when relatively large numbers of the masses are mobilized, militarized, and used as a means of coercion against the Other, who are often represented by the more marginalized demographics. Nationalist and fanatic mobilizations around racist and sectarian identities result in the reproduction of inter-societal and cross-societal violence. The elites who control the

DOI: 10.4324/9781003351429-3

means of the culture industry are to be blamed for the false consciousness that makes the economically exploited commit violence against those who are exploited economically and demonized racially and/or religiously at the same time. Even if a reader does not want to label forms of exclusionary politics I revisit here as "fascism," the main argument regarding the need for wider and more critical public debates about problematizing exclusionary ideologies, politics, and policies that perpetuate discrimination and violence remain sound. Also, the cases that are analyzed are actual rather than hypothetical, so the plausibility of the main point advanced is not contingent on any particular conceptual validity or invalidity. For instance, the critical analyses and conceptual applications of fascism as an ideology form might not be persuasive enough for traditional scholars of fascism. However, definitional disagreements about fascism do not affect the educational value of what the chapter shows in terms of the unjustified cases of discrimination and what the chapter argues for, namely the imperativeness of the critique of all cases of unjustified discrimination.

The problem (of fascism or whatever it may be called) is not unique to any particular nationality, ethnicity, or religious sect. Any perceived identity, such as Turkish, Arab, Persian, Kurdish, Sunni, Shia, or Sufi, that is the identity of perpetuators of violent oppression of others in a particular temporospatial context can very well be the perceived identity of the victims of violent oppression in another temporospatial context. Of course, in the world of nation-states, the stateless are more prone to be subjected to fascist violence. That said, there is nothing in victimhood or statelessness that would rule out the possibility of the rise of fascism among former victims or former stateless groups. In fact, if anything, narratives of victimhood are often used as effective in-group justifications for advancing the group's own fascist ideologies and practices especially within the frame of an assumed political sovereignty. *There* is a high probability of fascism being born and grown domestically but unnoticeably among the previously colonized groups. It is not improbable for fascist movements to emerge even among currently colonized groups especially when that group identifies with a broader, expansionist, and imperialist identity whether on the basis of religious or ethnic politics.

Finally, fascist elites in MENA *have been* exploiting the false culturalist dichotomy of West-East to disguise their continual violation of the rights and dignities of the ruled majority in their countries. More to the point, by exploiting the oversimplified but common anti-imperialist discourse and the moralist Eurocentric belief according to which imperialism is exclusively associated with whiteness, fascist elites in MENA have been able to advance their imperialist, racist, and at times even genocidal agenda in the name of resisting Western imperialism. Meanwhile, the post-Marxist left in the West has for the most part believed the culturalist lie of racism. In the 1970s, the left, for instance in West Germany, had no problem calling the Shah of Iran a fascist. Today, thanks to the widespread culturalization of politics and politicization of culture (Ahmed 2022a, also see Chapter 5 of this book), both the left and the right in the West seem to believe that Khamenei is indeed the supreme spiritual leader of Iranians and that he is indeed fighting Western imperialism. Meanwhile, for the last 40 years, Iranians from all backgrounds have tried everything not only to show their rejection of the ruling regime but also to bring it down. Even armed struggle has continued throughout the last 43 years, yet in this culturalist era, it has become possible not to hear Iranians and instead believe a ruling elite that is by all accounts criminal (Amnesty International 2017). Similarly, under Erdogan's ruling party (Amnesty International 2020; HRW 2021), democratic and progressive voices have been persecuted especially during the last ten years. However, Erdogan's claim to collective/cultural representation and his appeal to the culturalist mentality outside Turkey have been by far more effective than the plight of the oppressed in Turkey, including Turks and Muslims not to mention Kurds and non-Muslims. Even when thousands of scholars and educators were persecuted across Turkey and many were forced to escape the country to the West, boycotting Erdogan's regime was never considered in the European and American civil society associations, to say nothing about governments.

Fascist Ideologies, Geographies, and Phases

Fascism cannot be conceptually circumscribed exclusively to any particular region or nationality. Nor can the scholarly investigation of it be tasked exclusively to any particular academic discipline. Therefore, fascism should be approached as a multidisciplinary and interdisciplinary open-ended problem. Moreover, as I have argued in an article:

> critically examining the *form* of an ideology is sufficient to determine whether the ideology is fascist or not, regardless of the content of the ideology in terms of its particular similarities or dissimilarities, agreement or disagreement, with the doctrines of any other fascist ideology, including Italian Fascism and German Nazism
>
> (Ahmed 2023b, 676).

> Whether the essentialized Other in the ideology is Jew, Arab, Muslim, black, Catholic, Asian, white, Chinese, or some sort of combination such as Native American women, Somali men, or Latin American immigrants, matters only insofar as we study the particularity of a specific case of fascism
>
> (Ahmed 2023b, 676).

While the theory of "ideology form" is helpful to diagnose some of the contemporary Western forms of fascism that acquired new discursive strategies of democratic camouflaging, in the Middle East, for better or worse, the forms of fascism remain to have clear affinities with the older forms of fascism, which are openly racist and vulgarly antagonistic to the essentialized and homogenized Other. The broadly justified principle of armed struggle against colonialism resulted in the domination and continuation of the language of violence in the political spaces and public spheres across MENA. In contrast to communist parties who emphasized the politicization of the working class and the construction of a proletarian class consciousness that, at least from their viewpoint, would inherently be democratic, the nationalist parties increasingly undermined the role of the civil society and the foundational principles of democratic participation replacing the paradigm of class and its objective denominators with the paradigm of "the nation." This in turn helped mystify all the crucial loci of political power. Suddenly, as it were, it became morally and politically acceptable to use excessive force against every movement of dissent, brutalize entire populations in the name of national unity and security, and, in short, create a political world in which the exercise of power is universalized producing monster states strongly tied to the interests and fate of oppressive governments. In the meantime, even those who in the name of emancipation founded armed struggle movements to, whether rightly or wrongly, fight their colonizers started to sanctify violence. Specially in the 1970s and later, across the Arab world, a great deal of literature, music, and visual arts started to glorify the image of an assault rifle gun and the Palestinian fighter. Legendary singers such as Umm Kulthum and Fairuz sang about war with the same, if not more, passion with which they sang about romantic love. Their voices, along with the voices of countless poets, novelists, play writers, and other intellectuals, had an immeasurably profound effect on millions of young men and women, many of whom would readily see in this new enemy, Israel, the cause for all their sexual, emotional, social, and political disappointments. Quickly, the image of the general, the national hero, the father figure who will supposedly come to reinstall the lost glories of the ancient times gained extraordinary psychic powers over millions of *mobomassified* people rendering any talk of class consciousness obsolete among large sections of the working class from Iraq and Syria to Morocco and Algeria.

In the 1970s, a similar wave of romanticization of guns, shooting at the enemy, and the image of Peshmerga proliferated in Kurdish lyrics, plays, novels, and songs in Iraq and Iran. To this day, even after 32 years of the deeply corrupt and oppressive peshmerga rule in parts of Iraqi Kurdistan, the word peshmerga remains for the large part sanctified especially among Iranian Kurds, which is a sad commentary on the reproduction of violence vertically and horizontally in the Kurdish society and personality in the name of resistance. Somehow, the image of the armed man took over the general imagination rendering every aspect of political, communal, and intellectual life secondary to the appeal of guns. Sadly, the state violence that was supposed to be resisted has given birth to a world exclusively signified in terms of the symbolism of violence.

To return to the Palestinian case, even a group like Hamas, which has repeatedly proved that it does not have the slightest regard for Palestinian lives, remains widely exempted from any critique across most of the Arab media. Any critique of Hamas is immediately dismissed as siding with the Israeli colonial project. Under the Hamas rule in Gaza, it is understandable why more Palestinians do not speak up against Hamas's devastating politics, but, unfortunately for the Gazans, it is mostly those who do not live under Hamas (and do not experience what Gazans go through) that sanctify Hamas as a movement of resistance. What is even more disturbing is the fact that there is a near complete absence of a minimal level of rational argumentation in the public sphere to assess Hamas's acts. Hamas's strategy of hostage taking is simply based on two premises: 1- Israel does not give up on the lives of its citizens, and 2- Palestinian lives have little value for Hamas. Only with these two premises deeply rooted in the Islamist mentality of Hamas's leadership can that leadership's catastrophic decisions be explained. This is why to the Hamas leaders taking any number of Israeli hostages is worth the loss of tens of thousands of Palestinian lives.

In the war Hamas started on October 7, 2023, within less than 60 days, more than 3 percent of the residents of the Gaza Strip lost their lives, many more were injured, and about 80 percent were displaced. Some days, within 24 hours, the number of Palestinian civilians who were killed was twice the number of the Israeli hostages in Hamas's captivity.[1] Based on Hamas's own reports, on average 200 Palestinians were killed per day by Israeli fire (Elaph 2024), not to mention Palestinians who lost their lives because of the collapse of the health system and starvation and those who were injured for life. None of that made the Hamas leadership release the 120–130 Israeli hostages. On the contrary, had Hamas intentionally collaborated with the ultra-right Israeli elements to ensure the destruction of Gaza, it would not have acted any better for that purpose. Ultimately, the Netanyahu right-wing government took military steps to destroy life conditions in most of the enclave. At the same time, Egypt, Jordan, and other states made sure the Palestinians who were trapped in Gaza would not be able to leave the enclave despite months of continual bombardment, starvation, and homelessness.

Hamas is not unique in its complete disrespect for the lives of the people it supposedly defends. All Islamist movements disrespect human lives, especially the lives of the people who are unfortunate enough to be under their rule. In fact, the problem in many ways exceeds Islamist movements to also include secular nationalist movements in the Middle East, as the long list of dictators have proven over decades. There is a problem in MENA, and the problem might be better diagnosed if we look into the notion and history of fascism. Whether or not exclusionary movements discussed in this book should be called fascist is of secondary importance. The main point of this chapter is that without problematizing ideological forms that celebrate violence and fanatically reject otherness, exclusionism will most likely continue to be part of the political scene for a long time to come. Indeed, even in its classical sense, fascism has never been widely problematized anywhere among the Middle Eastern and North African intelligentsia or academia. I think new intellectual, academic, and public conventions should be established precisely to interrogate every nationalist and religious political front from an anti-fascist perspective. Hopefully, problematizing fascism on multiple levels will prepare the path to a world where the individual right to life and freedom is sanctified and Otherness is strongly protected.

The Rise of Fascism

The rise of fascism in Europe in the twentieth century was not merely due to an unfortunate turn of events in the 1920s and 1930s; rather, as Horkheimer and Adorno realized in their co-authored masterpiece, *Dialectic of Enlightenment* (2002), it was a historical point at which the political power of the reactionary forces that started to take shape and momentum right from the beginning of the Enlightenment project reached its peak forming a decisive front against progressive cosmopolitan forces that descended from the Enlightenment project. The Middle Ages already had prepared sufficient grounds for chauvinism and political anti-Semitism to give birth to something as violent and catastrophic as Nazism. That is also to say, while nationalism comes to the stage in the late modernity, it is only reasonable to think of its roots in the earlier centuries not so much as the Hegelian notion of the progression of reason but precisely as a turning point in the development of regression, unreason, at times as a continuation of the religious irrationality and at times as a reaction to the revolutionary project of the Enlightenment. Therefore, blaming the Enlightenment as such, as is fashionable now due to both wrong-headed versions of postmodernism and the rise of religiosity, is precisely an expression of the persisting irrationality, which amounts to the ultimate submission to the age of fascism as the ultimate end of history. As the Frankfurt School critical theorists insisted, instrumental rationality is at the heart of fascism, and it is the Enlightenment that gave birth to such an irrational rationality. However, it is crucial to emphasize that the Frankfurters remained faithful to the progressive Marxist doctrine, and as such they were careful not to commit any romanticization of the Middle Ages including and especially the political influence of religion.

While fascism was undeniably an outcome of the European nationalism, which in turn emerged from the Enlightenment project, fascism did not amount to the ultimate end of the Enlightenment project. In other words, despite the rational unjustifiability of any attempt to attribute some sort of an emancipatory teleological inner rationality to historical events that include Auschwitz, in the very will of the survivors themselves the bright side of the Enlightenment endured. Thus, the fascist era did not mean all hope was lost with the Enlightenment project. If anything, "for the sake of the hopeless ones" to use Walter Benjamin's phrase (2004, 356), for the sake of the victims of reactionary forces including fascism, we have no other option but to continue the struggle.

Europe has something tangible, namely the catastrophic rise of Fascism and Nazism, to lean on in order to reach the shores of a non-fascist, non-tribalist, and rational world. Unfortunately, it has not succeeded as it betrayed the most fundamental principles of the Enlightenment by tribally walling itself. To add insult to injury, today Europe relies on mercenaries and states that use mercenaries to guard its gates against the non-White Other. Today the values of the Enlightenment project are desperately fought for in the cities of

Afghanistan, Turkey, Syria, Iran, Egypt, and Sudan, rather than European and American institutions. However, in order to defend such a polemical claim and shed light on the significance of relatively popular but extremely underrepresented social movements in the MENA region, we need to comprehend the nature and scope of the challenges facing the oppressed majority in the region. For that purpose, this book focuses on the crisis of fascism in the MENA region.

Fascist idealogues in the Middle East have not been compelled to disguise their aggressive racist and extremist worldviews. Rather, for the most part, the dominant ideologies continue to be discursively vulgar and openly violent. Since its historical emergence in the first half of the twentieth century, fascism has never ceased to be prominent among nationalist elites in the Middle East. For the most part, the frenzy of nationalism that was intensified by European colonialism and European invention of nation-states created a landscape in which fascism was the natural outcome. Long centuries of the hegemony of religious orthodoxy, patriarchal domination, and widespread violence against the underprivileged only further normalized the fascist political climate of post-European-colonial era. Of course, there are often significant differences from one regime to another, but many of them have fascism, as an *ideology form*, in common.

It just so happened that at the end of the WWI an Italian right-winger would coin the term and Mussolini's movement would proclaim to be Fascists (with a capital F). By the 1930s, the term was used to describe similar ultra-right-wing movements elsewhere in Europe. When the Axis camp lost WWII, the term almost completely fell out of popularity and gradually became a derogatory one for most people.[2] Even at the peak of the interwar fascist era, most fascists outside of Europe, including Japan, never actually identified themselves as such. However, this did not prevent political theorists from labeling the Japanese regime of the 1930s as fascist. In the Middle East, the dominant ideologies of the ruling groups are fascist par excellence, even by conventional standards of fascism studies. They are racist, ultra-nationalist, puritan, chauvinist, totalitarian, anti-individualist, anti-liberal, anti-communist, intolerant of minorities, violent, expansionist, exclusionary, irrational, and often apocalyptic. They glorify violence, sanctify racist wars, deploy extreme populism, metaphysicalize the "national" identity, dehumanize and demonize otherness, popularize myths and mysticism, appeal to the *mobomasses*,[3] idolize the father figure, continually produce images of conspiring enemies, and victimize the collective (ethnic and/or religious) self. The ultranationalist and Islamist discourses systematically call for the unity among all in-groups to uproot imagined internal enemies and defeat fictive external enemies. Precisely because these are so common among the ruling regimes and the elite groups that support those regimes in the Middle East, fascism has not been problematized or criticized.

Like many other scholars, I am careful not to write what could be used to further the daily and systematic discrimination against Muslims wherever they might face discrimination as a minority. Ironically, American White supremacists and European neofascist movements commonly use the expression "Islamofascism." I believe it is crucially important for the public to realize that White supremacist ideology and Islamism belong to the same category despite the fact that each side, usually, not always, points to the other side to induce fear and hatred on which their own popularity depends for the most part. Fascism studies should play its role in clarifying that just as Aryan fascism is a political ideology that cannot be generalized to all Whites, Islamism is an ideology that is not endorsed by the majority of Muslim believers. Not despite but because of that, we are in need for serious fascism studies that could address Islamism in its various ideological, social, and political genealogies.

Avoiding the subject of fascism, whether religious or secular, would only make the despicable racist charges against millions of people more, not less, probable. In the meantime, religious authorities, whether Islamic, Christian, or Hindu, must not be sanctified wherever they commit discrimination against any particular population. The general English reader needs to realize that Muslim, Islamic, and Islamist are different terms with different references. As intelligent beings, we are capable of rejecting two wrongs at the same time. We can, and should, reject anti-Muslim neofascism and Islamism at the same time just as we should be able to reject anti-Christian violence and Christian fascism at the same time. Without such awareness, there is always the risk of supporting a fascist camp in the name of fighting fascism, which is also one of the issues I address in several contexts in this book.

Even when it comes to Islamist fundamentalism, the mainstream liberal and left in the West has refused to go beyond the habit of perceiving everything that has to do with Islam as the Other of the West. While the perception on the surface claims altruism and sympathy when the Muslim Other is systematically portrayed as a victim of the European man, it is deeply orientalist and Eurocentric for it is not able to recognize the subjective autonomy of the perceived Muslim or the simple fact that a Muslim majority society, like other societies, contains various right-wing and left-wing orientations, politics, and forces.

As a result, the far-right white nationalists and Islamophobes are left to freely exploit and abuse this gap that is caused by the lack of critical studies and formation of proper political alliances with the liberal, progressive, feminist, and democratic forces of the MENA region. Instead, often well-intended White liberals and leftists unknowingly fall into the trap of supporting fascist movements and regimes in the MENA region, assuming they are standing in solidarity with the victims of Western imperialism whereas the dissidents of the MENA region who live in a Western diaspora are often alienated and sometimes forced to become part of the White right-wing platforms in the West, whether out of political frustration or financial desperation.

There is a desperate need for critical studies of fascism that will not exclude the MENA region. The fact that there are, relatively speaking, only a few studies in this area is itself alarming. Limiting fascism studies geographically to Europe and the Europeanized world may, superficially, suggest Euro-self-critique, i.e., holding Europeans alone responsible for fascism. On a closer analysis, we should be able to realize that such a view, just like clearer forms of Eurocentrism, is problematic. The implied assumption is that non-Europeans do not have a superiority myth. This might sound alright until we raise questions such as, "why is such an assumption made in the first place?" and "what makes non-White societies immune to the emergence of supremacist ideologies, supposedly?" It seems to me that the Eurocentrism of fascism studies is rooted in a rather racist assumption according to which only Europeans can suffer from a racist arrogance, implying that non-Europeans cannot be even fascists.

It is definitely not that other societies are assumed to be free of confused, misguided, and irrational groups. It is just that even in *their* forms of confusion, misguidedness, and irrationality, as the unspoken assumption goes, they do not produce supremacy myths. And why not? This is where the mental racist structure can be exposed. Even though racist supremacy is always a myth, just like any other myth, it is the product of a false subjective reading of an objective reality. That is to say, the nature of the subjective falsity is still dependent on the nature of the objective reality. The only explanation for why it is assumed that non-Whites are not at risk of constructing superiority myths is that it is assumed that everyone in all non-White societies are always already living with an unmistakable sense of inferiority. Therefore, the unconscious prejudice beneath the politically correct assumption that fascism is a White-racist phenomenon is itself a White racist prejudice. To assume that fascism is a White phenomenon does not entail that non-Whites are universally and metaphysically so good that they would not produce fascist movements. Rather, the unconscious assumption is that the non-White cannot even be a fascist. After all, fascism is a political notion and as such to be fascist presupposes subjecthood, personhood, autonomous individuality, and the ability to be wrong.

Political terms are not attributed to beings who lack subjecthood, personhood, individuality, and autonomous faculties of judgment. We do not describe a cat or a horse as liberal, socialist, or fascist, for instance, simply because a cat or a horse is not a political actor. For the dominant Eurocentric modes of ideology, non-Europeans' social and political lives are traditionally and culturally determined just as the behavior of cats and horses are determined on bases other than autonomous faculties of rational and moral judgment.

Throughout the rest of the book, there will be other occasions to revisit this oblique form of racism, or culturalism, and further problematize it, but now an overview of fascism in the Middle East is in order. However, what follows is not a conventional account of political groups that identified themselves as fascists. Such an account would be based on the conventional definitions of fascism, which are not effective for diagnosing fascism beyond a particular history and geography (Ahmed 2023b). Moreover, the political weight of self-identified fascist groups in the Middle East has been negligible anyway; what is more important is to examine dominant movements and ideologies in search of symptoms of fascism, which is the objective of the rest of this chapter.

Fascism and the Middle East

Turkey

Turkish fascism actually predates both Italian and German fascism. This claim might sound odd to scholars who continue to consider Italian fascism the starting point of fascism, even though Italian fascism would not meet the most important criterion of fascism as defined by Giovanni Gentile himself, namely, totalitarianism (1995, 54). While Kemalism as a model of fascism has been largely ignored in fascism studies, finally a few illuminating works became available in the last ten years, including Stefan Ihrig's (2014) extensive and rigorous historiographic research that shows Kemalism's influence on Italian fascism and the formation of Nazism. Ihrig's work shows beyond any doubt that if we were to place the beginning of fascism in the twentieth century both as an ideology and a regime, it should be

Kemalism. The fact that Ataturk provided the first fascist example is clear even from direct references made by both Mussolini and Hitler. For instance, Mussolini called himself "the Mustafa Kemal of a Milanese Ankara" (qt. in Ihrig 2014, 106), and the fascist monthly *Gerarchia* headlined its last issue prior to the fascist March on Rome "*La luna crescent,*" which was the title of an article on "Kemal Pasha's March on Izmir" written by the Duce himself (Ihrig 2014, 106). Hitler proudly admitted this fact, for instance, when he said "Atatürk was a teacher; Mussolini was his first and I his second student" or "Turkey was our model" and Ataturk was a "star in the darkness" (qt. in Ihrig 2014, 116).

Vahram Ter-Matevosyan makes a strong case for criticizing the dismissal of the fascism of Kemalism in fascism studies (2015). Ter-Matevosyan bases his approach on Sternhell's account according to which the beginning of fascism in the history of ideas is the nineteenth century. Then, he traces back the origins of Pan-Turkism to the late nineteenth century when Turkish elites came under a heavy influence of German and French racist nationalists and social Darwinists (Ter-Matevosyan 2015), and by the turn of the century, nationalist "writers began to emphasize the superiority of the Turks over other, especially Muslim, Ottoman ethnic groups," (Hanioglu 2014, 9). Ter-Matevosyan then observes that:

> once in power from 1908 to 1918 (with a brief interlude in 1912) and particularly after 1913, the Committee for Union and Progress had the chance to experiment with some of the constitutive elements of the fascist ideology, although the word came into existence later
>
> (Ter-Matevosyan 2015, 213).

The fascist policies only intensified in the following decades both influencing and being influenced by Italian and German fascism, but even in the years prior to the establishment of the Turkish Republic, the nationalist movement succeeded in "spontaneous application of many policy features (Pan-Turkism, unification of all Turks to build the Turkish father-land, expansionist ambitions, homogenisation, assimilation, resettlement of population)" (Ter-Matevosyan 2015, 213).

Other than the invention of the name, there is barely anything in Italian Fascism in 1920–1921 that could render it a more developed form of fascism than Turkish fascism both then and now. In fact, one can argue that Mussolini's movement never made it to the level of hegemony, totalitarianism, militarization, and mass racist mobilization of society enjoyed by Turkish nationalism. Therefore, Hitler's claim that he and Mussolini had been Ataturk's disciples was anything but metaphoric. While the Duce's goal to revive the glories of the Roman Empire and the Führer's dream of a third Reich were semi-mythical at best, Kemal Pasha, who eventually named himself the Father of Turks, "Ataturk" in Turkish, was actually one of the generals of the Empire. However, he wanted a more homogeneous and modern state with one absolute will, language, and Pan-Turkish ideology led by himself. In other words, Kemalism was already incomparably a more developed fascist ideology than either Fascism or Nazism would ever become. Not to mention the fact that Ataturk's fascist regime and ideology are still alive and well after more than a century of its birth.

Today, thanks to Erdogan's neo-Ottoman amendments, Turkish fascism leads not only Pan-Turkic nationalism but also Sunni Islamism with a strong imperialist agenda stretching its colonialist ambitions from Central Asia to North Africa, from Italy's and France's former colonies to the gates of Europe itself. Also, very much like the Duce and the Führer, Erdogan shows little respect to anyone except for other powerful absolutists, such as Putin and Trump. In the meantime, Erdogan has successfully bullied the European political leaders, exploiting their xenophobia and bad faith in the universal human rights, to pay his regime billions of Euros in order to keep refugees outside Europe. Erdogan is a typical fascist leader especially in terms of his strategy to smash every perceived and potential opponent in the order of vulnerability starting from the most vulnerable, and to maximally exploit those who show signs of relative weakness. Therefore, he will continue to make the most out of Europe's bad faith. While his proxy wars and Islamist expansion continue to create more and more refugees, he makes himself increasingly indispensable as the only man who holds the key to the damn behind which there is what Europe perceives as the single most fatal threat, the "refugee flood." It seems as though the horrors of the 1529's siege of Vienna has not left Euro-imagination, but this time around the European leadership knowingly wants to mistake the victims for the invaders and Recep Tayyip Erdogan for John III Sobieski. Jihadis supported by Erdogan have been roaming around turning almost every civil war in the MENA region into another ISIS-like nightmare, while Islamophobic Europeans, without any sense of irony or guilt, continue to support Turkey with money, military logistics, and weapons.

Chauvinism is a core characteristic of every fascist ideology, but the rise of fascism is a cross-national and cross-continental phenomenon.

Fascist movements enable each other by capitalizing on and exploiting various provincial, racist, and sectarian xenophobia. The point to be emphasized here is not just that fascism has never left the Middle East since its inception but also Europe has never securely moved beyond fascism. The racist distrust of the Muslim Other of Europe has fulfilled the xenophobic prophesy by empowering Islamists and creating millions of refugees. At the same time, that very mentality has contributed to the realization of the worst possible outcomes for Europe's perceived Other. Namely, it has further disempowered the victims of Islamism, i.e., the vast majority of ordinary people in the MENA region, including those who become refugees escaping violence and its consequences.

By the 1930s, Kemalism "introduced the absolute superiority of 'Turkishness' (understood as something in between Nation and Race) and its revolution; which, in turn, legitimized the pyramidal rule of the Chiefs, headed by the Eternal Chief" (Bozarslan 2014, 34), and Kemal Ataturk had already become the worshiped figure whose images had occupied the foci of all public spaces. The racist policies of Turkification and the Kemalist personality cult as two clear signs of Turkish fascism still continue in Turkey, only supplemented by religious fanaticism and neo-Ottoman imperialism under Erdogan.

The Armenian genocide provided the model for the Nazis' determinate intention to commit the Holocaust (Ihring 2014). As the head of the state and the idealized absolute leader of Turkish nationalism, in the 1930s, Kemal Ataturk, had the Turkish scientists publish biological research supposedly proving superiority of the Turkish race (Hanioglu 2011, 162–171). Kemalism waged its genocidal campaigns against all those who were not considered Turks in Anatolia long before Nazism became popular in Germany, and the enduring power of fascist discourse in Turkey's political sphere suggests that it has largely outlived Nazism and other European fascist regimes. Unlike Nazism, Turkish fascism has continued to enjoy virtually uninterrupted support from Western democracies. The West tends to view Kemalism against the Islamic Middle Eastern backdrop, as opposed to the liberal European milieu. From that perspective, all that matters ideologically is that Kemalism stands out as both secular and pro-Western. The continual genocidal campaigns against non-Turkish Anatolian peoples, most notably Armenians, but also Assyrians, Yezidis, Greeks (from 1915–1923), and later Kurds (starting with the Zaza and Alevi Kurds of Dersim in 1937–1938) have never been factored into Western democracies' diplomatic calculations. While the rise of the French National Front and the Freedom Party of Austria have, understandably, spurred panic throughout Europe, Turkey remains an indispensable ally of Europe and the US. Of course, Western complicity over the last century has only served to further legitimize and normalize Turkish fascism.

Just as in Italy until the 1940s and in Spain until the 1970s, in Turkey, anti-fascist Marxist and other leftist social movements have always been strongly present despite the violent suppression to which they have been subjected since the 1920s. Most recently, with the emergence of the Peoples' Democratic Party (HDP), a new movement has appeared that is supported by progressive Kurds, Turks, Arabs, Alevis, Christians, and others, which may be a hopeful historical turn whereby all forms of exclusionary discrimination are challenged in the interest of an inclusive political environment and an egalitarian social climate. The HDP is the only political party that 1.- enjoys a relative popularity in not only the Kurdish majority cities but also in some Turkish majority cities, and, at the same time, 2.- explicitly rejects fascism and all forms of discrimination, including discrimination against politically oppressed peoples such as Kurds and Armenians, and discrimination against societally marginalized groups such as women, children, and LGBTQ+. The HDP is part of a larger movement in Turkey, which is in turn part of an even broader regional post-national movement that is uniquely egalitarian, inclusive, feminist, secular, and pluralist. The Rojava experiment in Syria is the strongest manifestation of the same movement.[4] Recently, that same movement's central slogan, *Jin, Jiyan, Azadi* (women, life, freedom), has been adopted by the popular Iranian anti-regime protest movement that (in less than two weeks after its first spark following the killing of a Kurdish woman, Mehsa Jina Amini, in Tehran at the hands of the regime's morality police), in addition to the Kurdish majority Kurdistan, reached every corner of the country including, the Persian majority area in the center, the Arab majority of Arabistan, the Baluchi Majority of Baluchistan, and the Azeri majority of Western Azerbaijan. Given these promising signs of what seems to be a new internationalist popular movement of resistance, despite the endurance of some old fascist forces and the rise of new ones, the MENA region could indeed enter a post-national or *postnihilist* era.

The Arab World

Turkish nationalism also inspired the "spiritual father of Arab nationalism" Sati Al-Husri who was an Ottoman official and a fanatic supporter of the Young Turks (Tibi 1997). Al-Husri (in)famously drew from the ideology of the Young Turks to cultivate Arab nationalism in Syria and Iraq, particularly in his fascist constructing of the education systems. During WWII, he openly advocated for the Nazis in the Arab world. In April 1941, with the help of Mussolini and Hitler's regimes, Al-Husri's followers in the Iraqi army carried out a military coup against the monarchy in Iraq and installed Rashid Ali al-Gailani who was also a pro-Nazi pan-Arabist. Al-Gailani's regime was removed in May by the Regent of Iraq, Abd al-Ilah with the help of the British forces (Tibi 1997, 121). However, this fascist coup gave rise to the bloodiest campaigns of the twentieth century against Iraqi Jews in Baghdad up until then. The nationalists accused the Jews of aiding the British army in retaking Baghdad and they mobilized the masses who attacked Jewish families across Baghdad killing hundreds of Jews and looting Jewish properties in the infamous pogrom known as *Farhud*, to which most other ethnic and religious groups would be subjected during the decades that followed. Al-Gailani fled to the Nazi Germany and Al-Husri was deported to Syria. However, Al-Husri became the most influential figure in shaping the Arab League from its early days in mid 1940s and the engineer of nationalizing the education systems in both Syria and Iraq (Tibi 1997, 121–122), both of which remain extremely fascist, among other things, in their portrayal of world history, international politics, Arabhood, and its adoption of anti-Semitism.

Jamal Abdul Nasser and the founders of Baathism were the next generation of Arab nationalists, after Al-Husri's generation. Egypt, especially under the celebrated Nasser, became a welcoming refuge for surviving Nazi officials. As Del Boca and Giovana explain, many Nazi officials who came to Egypt were even given prestigious and influential positions in the government (1970). Most notably, Nasser hired Johann von Leers, a major Nazi ideologue and propagandist, as his own adviser, who thought Nasser made a better leader than Hitler (Del Boca and Giovani 1970, 401). Praising Nasser's fascism, the French fascist Maurice Bardèche wrote:

> Nasser and his friends have discovered that the whole of Fascist mysticism is to be found in Islam, which is their past and, in the wider and more comprehensive sense of the term, their culture – that is to say, not only their source of inspiration, but something that conforms very closely with their nature and their instincts … Although it is just as inimitable as Hitler's Germanism, Nasser's crusade is, like National Socialism, confined to the men of one nation. But its geographical situation and the moment of its

> emergence endow it with the greatest significance. Of all the Fascist mysticisms it is probable the one which will leave the deepest mark on history on account of its enduring consequences
> (qt. in Del Boca and Giovana 1970, 401–402).

Ironically, here we witness a relatively early instance of the Post-WWII culturalism, only used to make the racist case in a fatally positive sense. Apparently, to Maurice Bardèche, the perceived Arab primitiveness makes Arabs more successful material for the fascist project. The liberal antithesis of this view completely excludes Arabs from fascism studies assuming that fascism is a European phenomenon. But we should not miss the irony here: both views are Eurocentric and racist because both are premised on the deeply rooted mentality of cultural racism. That is to say, the contrast between the two seemingly opposing positions is superficial. The difference simply stems from the two different political platforms or agenda, of European fascism and European liberalism, respectively. While Bardèche sees in Arabs natural fascists in need of some organization and mobilization, which was, allegedly, taken care of by Nasser, the liberal position is not prepared to elevate the perceived barbarity of Arabs to the level of the ideological sophistication of fascism. Since fascism is indeed a modern phenomenon, reaching modernity, even in the reactionary sense, is a necessary prerequisite for forming fascism. Because Arab societies are perceived to be pre-modern, it is assumed that no movement in those societies can obtain the ideological sophistication of fascism, or other forms of post-Enlightenment ideologies for that matter. Thus, at the root of both views, culturalism is strongly present. Needless to say, for that precise reason, among others, both views are false – contemporary Arab societies, like all contemporary societies, are exposed to the spectrum of modern ideologies from the far right to the far left, of course with respective geopolitical specifications. In my work, including this book, I aim to problematize and refute culturalism in all its implicit and explicit, illiberal and liberal, antagonistic and moralistic, applications, thereby rejecting the false dichotomies produced by Eurocentrism. Regardless of its geographic and historical circumstances, a society must neither be demonized nor romanticized. When nationalism became the dominant ideological form of the age, Arabs, like Turks, Persians, and others, were not an exception. Also, like other nationalisms, Arab nationalism produced its own fascist tendencies.

Nasserism's rivals in Syria and Iraq were the Baathists.[5] Both Nasser's Arab Socialist Union and the Arab Socialist Baath Party relied heavily on the German National Socialist model not only in their propaganda (Goebbels is still quoted by Baathists), but also in their anti-Semitic discourse, depictions of the leader as the savior destined to restore the glory of the nation, and, of course, calls for national purity and a "final solution" for all those who failed to meet the nationalist criteria. In fact, concentration camps for political dissidents, defectors, rivals, and minorities figured prominently in the Baathist regime in Iraq. The regime perfected the politics of elimination by completely erasing every trace of all the victims of *Anfal* in the late 1980s. As far as I know, to date, not a single picture of any of those concentration camps has been found, and no former Baathist soldiers have revealed any information about the methods used to eliminate so many people.

The Islamist and secular Arab nationalist alliance with Nazism has yet to be renounced in the Arab world, and anti-Semitism has arguably increased since the 1940s, as it is clear to any observer of the region's dominant political and religious discourses in which often Zionists and Jews are used interchangeably and sometimes Zionism, used vaguely, is the main object of antagonism.[6] Arab nationalists and Islamists have been exploiting the Israeli-Palestinian conflict from its very beginning to further justify and popularize their anti-Semitism among ordinary citizens.[7] While some of those who remember their Jewish neighbors look back nostalgically to the past, few Middle Easterners outside Israel have had any contact with Jews because most Jews were forced to leave their countries in the end of the 1940s and early 1950s. Therefore, for the growing up generation of the 1960s and later, there was nothing to counter the official anti-Semitic discourse that targeted Jews universally holding them responsible not only for the statelessness state of the Palestinian but also for more or less the continual state of crises whether wars, civil unrest, or economic under development and poverty. Perhaps what is most indicative of this typical anti-Semitic mentality, according to which there is always at least a Jewish conspiracy at work, is the ironic phenomenon of rivals accusing each other of Zionism. The premise is that Zionism is the worst possible crime, so if party A succeeded in convincing the public that party B has an affiliation with Zionism, nothing more is needed to be done to make party B collapse automatically as a result of the public's unforgiving reaction.

Throughout the Arab Spring uprisings, one of the most common accusations made by governments against their opposition was the alleged Zionist plot carried out by the traitors in order to destabilize the nationalist and patriotic government that proudly stood in the face of Zionist plans (Al-Labwani 2019). Similarly, the opposition would regularly accuse the rulers of working for Zionist interests and thereby securing the support of Israel and American imperialism (see, for instance, Hamdi 2013). Secular elites, including national socialists, and Islamists are usually fatal enemies, but they have anti-Semitism, and other forms of racism, in common. The movements of the Arab Spring did not change that anywhere from Tunisia to Yemen. By drawing attention to the disturbingly widespread anti-Semitism I do not mean to attribute fascism to the majority of ordinary people. Rather, I think the Arab intelligentsia is mainly to be blamed for consciously advocating fascist ideologies, in some cases, and for not problematizing fascism, in other cases. The problem is that if anything the anti-Semitic policies of Nazism made it more, not less, popular among opinion makers in the region. The degree to which fascism is not problematized by the intelligentsia and the normalcy of unmistakable anti-Semitic fascism exceeds the boundaries of academic concerns and jargons.

I made a conscious choice not to discuss the Israeli-Palestinian conflict and its role in spreading anti-Semitism for the simple fact that I do not want to contribute to the mentality that dismisses the magnitude of the problem of anti-Semitism by falsely associating its origin to that conflict. The mentality that searches for reasons in the deeds of the victims, or those rightly or wrongly associated with the victims, is itself a racist mentality. Racism always entails self-justification, and that justification is always false. Certainly, the Israeli-Palestinian conflict has intensified anti-Semitism among opinion makers in the Arab societies, but we should be able to address the problem of anti-Semitism without necessarily making that conflict part of the research. The Nazis strongly believed their anti-Semitic policies were a reaction to, or rather a solution for, what Jews allegedly had committed, or "the Jewish question." Today, the anti-Semitic mentality has not changed in terms of blaming the victims or those associated with them, or else anti-Semitism would have long ended. The Jews who were brutalized, robbed, or murdered in 1941 and those who were hanged on the electric poles of Baghdad in 1969 were as Baghdadis as anyone could be and had nothing to do with Israeli politics and policies (note that the state of Israel was founded in 1948). The same goes for the many millions of others from various nationalities and backgrounds, including Arabs and Muslims, who became victims of the same fascism over the decades that followed.

That said, perhaps this deep anti-Jewish sense of enmity will start to change if the most recent diplomatic normalization projects between

Israel and some Arab monarchies succeed in creating a shift in the public climate of opinion in Arab societies. What makes this somewhat probable is the fact that both Baathism and Nasserism, as the two extremist versions of Arab nationalism, have lost the popularity they enjoyed for many decades. Ironically, the Arab monarchies, including the Saudis, and with the exception of Qatar, have created a front against Islamism while Baathists, once adamantly secular and anti-Islamist, have joined the two main Islamist camps. Iraqi Baathists almost entirely have merged in Sunni Islamist movements, and the Syrian Baath sold its soul (along with the Syrian state sovereignty) to the Iranian Islamist regime and Hezbollah. Arab nationalist elites, whether secular or Islamist, have lost their leadership to the Islamist camps led by Erdogan's Ankara and Khamenei's Tehran. The bloody conflicts in both Syria and Yemen, show the hegemony of non-Arab players. In Yemen, the Houthis openly represent the Iranian regime's front against the Yemenis supported by the Kingdom of Saudi Arabia and the United Arab Emirates. In Syria, while the regime is supported by Iran, the Sunni Arab opposition has become a Turkish proxy fighting other Syrians to annex more land to the Turkish ruled territories. These are indications of the ultimate failure of Arab nationalism to reach any of its goals regarding national sovereignty, and Arab unity, let alone the revival of what to the nationalist mindset was once an Arab civilization. Not surprisingly, once more, those who want to make it great again have only succeeded in bringing about catastrophes, mass murder, suffering, and humiliation for their societies.

Under fascism, the Other is seen as an obstacle that must be neutralized, even if that means physical elimination. The majority's language, culture, and values are of course seen as natural and universal, at least within the geographic borders claimed by fascist nationalists. In stark contrast, the language, culture, and identity of the Othered minority, are considered sectarian, tribal, backward, strange, irrational, primitive, and so on. Thus, when the majority imposes its language and values on minorities, it is only for the sake of the minority's interest, supposedly. Unfortunately, this way of thinking continues to be indicative of how minorities are treated throughout the Middle East.

The minority is always expected to accept oppression unconditionally in order to demonstrate that they are not conspiring to overthrow the glorious nation, or simply to prove that they deserve the right to live. It is as though the minority's only task in life is to painstakingly try to win the ruling elites' trust. Yet, it is virtually impossible for the nationalist elites to ever really trust certain minorities, if for no other reason than because one "bad" action by a minority member is deemed representative of the entire minority group – while there is a tendency to underestimate the magnitude and significance of systematic acts of violence against minorities. And since it is sociologically impossible for all members of a minority group to act in the same "harmless" way, it is impossible to meet the (politicized) majority's conditions for earning trust.

The majority-minority relationship is very much analogous to the husband-wife relationship in the most misogynistic of societies. Typical of Middle Eastern fascism, fascist leaders often try to evoke familial emotions to both agitate the largest possible number of people among the majority and appease minorities. Because family is the locus of suppression in patriarchal societies, it makes sense to see state fascism as a broader development of the micro-fascist and chauvinist dynamics of the family. A particularly demonstrative example can be seen in Iraq, where Iraqi nationalist elites have responded to calls for independence in the Kurdistan region by repeatedly analogizing Kurdistan to the wife who seeks separation from her husband (Arab Iraq). Notably, this analogy is never phrased the other way around, which highlights how Kurds have been seen all along by nationalist Iraqi Arab elites. Just as the wife in a patriarchal society is habitually exploited and abused but is nonetheless expected to fully accept the authority of her husband, Kurds and other minorities in the Middle East are expected to bear the brunt of fascist regimes without complaint.

On September 25, 2017, Iraqi Kurds voted for independence in a referendum that was vehemently opposed by not only the Iraqi government but also the Turkish, Iranian, and Syrian governments. On the following day, an Iraqi newspaper called Al-Nahar, on its front page, published a picture of five black men in underwear standing behind a couch and staring at the young blond girl sitting on the couch. The image clearly indicated that the girl was about to be raped by the five men. The word printed on the chest of each one of the men read, Iran, Syria, Turkey, Iraq, and Jordon, respectively while the word "Kurdistan" was printed on the image of the female figure. Notice the newspaper used the image of five black men, which speaks to another layer of racist stereotypes at work, namely depicting black men as instruments of rape. The message, of course, was that Kurdistan was about to be raped by the five countries. Most of the remaining space on the page was dedicated to headlines and columns that indicated Turkish and Iraqi threats against Kurdistan.[8]

The state of Baluchis in Iran and Pakistan, the Amazigh in Morocco, and native Africans in Sudan and Mauritania are just a few other examples of nations whose very existence is seen as a threat to the imperial nation-states that oppress them. Asian and African countries immediately became imperialist at the very moments of their independence from their European colonizers. The assumption that the state is the political expression of the nation, which is in turn imagined to be culturally homogeneous and "racially" pure, has not been challenged widely enough in the region. During the period between the two world wars and the 1950s, communist movements represented the only relatively popular anti-fascist force throughout the region. Then, the brutal suppression of the communist parties along with Moscow's betrayal of the movement prepared the region for the reign of fascism unchallenged until the Arab Spring.

The Arab Spring, however, precisely because of the absence of a popular left was hijacked by Islamist forces almost in every case because they were the only movement that was organized enough to be able to determinately seize power, of course with the support of established Islamist regimes. During the first year of the Arab Spring, it already became clear that liberals would be neither able to seize power nor prepared to transform the uprisings to a revolution to rearrange the wider social relations of power and privilege. Islamism dominated the stage so swiftly that the Arab Spring was halted before reaching more than half of the Arab-majority countries. People had legitimate reason to cling to the existing autocratic regimes as opposed to opening the door for the Islamists whose kingdom of God was nothing but a common doomsday.

In times of crisis, which have been more or less continual throughout the Middle East over the last 100 years, the perception of stability is associated with the notion of a strong leader, a patriarch who can discipline everyone in the family. Fascist leaders, in turn, excel at playing the role of the father who can use excessive force, but only for the sake of everyone in the family, for creating unity and stability. Just like God, the leader is both merciless and merciful. When he appears to be too severe, it is only because he knows best. The leader does not have to explain anything because his wisdom is beyond the people's comprehension; his judgment is trusted as a matter of course.

Given the intellectual impoverishment of the fascist leader, this arrangement works perfectly well. The leader's strength lies in his manipulation of physical force, and whenever he speaks, his statements are easily quotable and relatable for the *mobomass* individual. With the passage of time, and surrounded by an ingratiating inner circle, the leader comes to believe the lie that he is a sort of divine being, which quickly gives him the confidence to talk about everything. The follower reads this development as the leader's incredible modesty, insofar as he is willing to engage with issues of concern to the average man. However, this habit of talking about everything is in fact a clear symptom of old fashion totalitarianism. Fascism is, as Giovani Gentile put it, "a total conception of life" (1995, 54). The leader, as the embodiment of divine wisdom, becomes the authority in all arenas of social life and knowledge. He could pass judgment on anything from personal hygiene and eating habits to clothing choices, raising children, education, ethics, and medicine.

Saddam Hussein, for instance, had no reservations about advising all women that they should shower twice a day. In the same speech, he would also make statements about imperialism, the enemies of the nation, and the glorious future the revolution would secure for the nation. Every word he uttered would be reported by the media as sacred text. In the same vein, Khomeini in his *Little Green Book*, which is a collection of his fatwas and is religiously esteemed by his faithful followers, unflinchingly provides detailed instructions for the proper way to defecate and clean oneself afterwards (Khomeini 1985, §21).

In the old versions of fascist ideologies, there is always a fascist figure who is treated as a divine being. Insulting this leader is considered a serious crime on the level of blasphemy, for he symbolizes everything the nation aspires to be. He is the teacher, the father, the leader, the philosopher, and, of course, the hero. He gazes at everyone in the nation through his images and statues positioned at the very center of public spaces. It is because of him – not the miserable marginalized souls who build the infrastructure, farm the land, and clean the streets – that the nation thrives. From birth he was fated for a sacred mission, for making the nation free and powerful. He is above and beyond mistakes or misdeeds.

The fascist leader symbolizes force, and it is typical of sadomasochistic personalities to identify with the powerful and resent the marginalized, as we learn from Wilhelm Reich (1970, 63). Identifying with the powerful amounts to disguising the broken personality that has suffered from prolonged humiliation and suppression. Crushed and degraded, the authoritarian character, "the personality structure which is the human basis of Fascism" in Fromm's words (1965, 186), perceives power as the magical redemption for everything, but above all power is the main path to negating their own feeling of insignificance. The fascist movement, regardless of its religiosity or secularism, offers the mobs a religious experience of euphoria and a sense of purpose. What makes this source of power and purpose especially appealing is that the fascist doctrine articulated by the leader is extremely simplistic, containing strong elements of mysticism. Expressions such as "the spirit of the nation" or "the greatness of the nation," as both Mussolini and Hitler were well-aware, designate nothing but a myth that is intended to stimulate the irrational drives of the followers. As such, they give rise to a violent movement eager to attack at the slightest provocation, which is usually supplied by the leadership and the fascist propaganda machine. The role of the charismatic leader is essential for mobilizing the mobs, which in turn is essential for the formation of fascist totalitarianism, Arendt noted (1979, xxxii).

The failure of Arab nationalism to fulfill any of its promises including the realization of Arab unity and emancipating Palestine has divided the popular bases of Pan-Arabism between the Sunni and Shia sectarian lines, which are exploited to their full political potentialities by the rulers of Turkey and Iran respectively. The retrogressive fallbacks into nationalism and then into Islamism were rooted in the demise of the communist movement, which was once a main if not the main emancipatory orientation in Egypt and Iraq. Relative to the size of the respective populations, the number of revolutionary communists in Egypt was substantially larger than the number of Bolsheviks in Russia on the eve of the October Revolution. The Iraqi Communist Party (ICP) was by far the most popular political party in the country until the Baathists took over power and banned political parties (Laqueur 1956, 277; Franzén 2011). In early 1959, the party leadership announced that they could not accept new members because they were simply overwhelmed by the large turnout (Farough-Sluglett and Sluglett 2001, 63). Bloody campaigns against the communists at the hands of police states from Tunisia, Egypt, and Sudan to Yemen, Syria, and Iraq continued for decades until the movement was almost eradicated, leaving the stage for two retroactive protagonists. Arab nationalism transfigured most of the Arab republics to what could be considered textbook cases of fascist dictatorships. Bashar Al-Assad is the last surviving member of that class of nationalist Arab leaders who have never failed to bring upon their peoples every imaginable form of division, suffering, and humiliation on multiple national, regional, and global levels. Baathism and Nasserism were the two main lines of Arab nationalism, and both were the equivalents of German national socialism. Nasserism started to lose its hegemony after Nasser's death in 1970 when Baathism had just started its absolutist reign in both Iraq and Syria. The Syrian Baath has been in power in Damascus since 1963, and Baghdad fell under Baathism from 1968 to 2003. Both Baath parties, in Syria and Iraq, kept their mother party's slogan: "A single Arab nation with an immortal mission." Today, the Iraqi and

Syrian societies are among the most devastated and brutalized societies in the world.

The moment the Baathist iron fist lost its grip, Sunni Islamism and Shia Islamism turned the two countries into a showcase of their kingdom of God, depriving the marginalized, including women, of even the limited personal freedoms they were granted during the Baathist reign. The Baathist rule continues in parts of Syria, including Damascus, but even in those areas, Islamist militias have changed the public space irrevocably. Today, the cities of Baghdad, Mosul, Aleppo, and Damascus live their darkest days arguably since Hulagu Khan's reign in the end of the sixth and beginning of the seventh decades of the thirteenth century.

The nationalist leader felt entitled to eternal authority due to his actual or alleged role in the anti-colonial past struggle and positioned himself as the new god on earth in a disturbingly fascist style that mixed republicanism with a prototypical notion of dynasticism, citizenship with the absolute oneness of "the nation," and patriotism with the unconditional allegiance to the oneness ultimately embodied by the leader (in the same way the king was believed to be an embodiment of divinity in Ancient Egypt and the Europe of the Middle Ages). The so-called post-colonial republics not only repeated the European experiment of nationalism but in many cases duplicated the worst, namely the fascist, models. More or less, from Iran and Turkey to Libya and Algeria, each republic had its own Führer or Il Duce with pictures and statues of him occupying the focal points of both public space (and private space, which could only ironically be called private thanks to the police regimes that expanded the frontiers of the exercise of power to all arenas including people's living rooms). Indeed, the leaders in the so-called republics were by far bloodier and more totalitarian than both the past and enduring traditional monarchies across MENA. In fact, also like Il Duce and the Führer, the nationalist leaders were most obsessed by their utter enmity against the internationalists of their respective countries and had no tolerance for those who were deemed unfit to be part of the great nation, whether in Turkey, Iran, or the Arab republics. While in Europe Italian Fascism and Hitler's Nazism were criminalized and problematized in the post-WWII era, in the MENA region, fascism continues in its old form. This is to say, fascists in the MENA region have not been compelled to shrink in size or somehow mask their openly racist language in the interest of an opaquer fascist discourse.[9]

Iran

Pan-Persian Aryanism is an evident case of the dominance and continuation of the inter-war model of fascism. While Pan-Turkish fascism gained momentum around the same time as Italian Fascism, and Pan-Arab fascism was under indirect influence of both Turkish nationalism and German Nazism, Persian fascism from the beginning was directly linked to Aryanism. In fact, Aryanism is still the normal discursive model in the Pan-Iranian intelligentsia. Iranian nationalists do not seem to see any issue with taking pride from the Persian so-called race's so-called Aryan origin. Even worse, in the Persian speaking public sphere, one gets the impression that there is no sense of concern regarding the political incorrectness of Aryanist mythology and rhetoric. References to the "Aryan race" constitutes the normative aspect of Pan-Iranian nationalism and patriotism. That said, luckily, there is a number of Iranian scholars whose works focus on problematizing this issue. The quantity of such works, in comparison to those who maintain the racist norm, is still extremely small, but hopefully their influence will increase quickly among the general Persian speaking Iranian intelligentsia. Below, I will touch on some the relevant works of anti-fascist critical research that are conducted by Iranian scholars.

Mostafa Vaziri's pioneering book, *Iran as Imagined Nation*, originally published in 1993, offers a comprehensive account of the mythology, orientalism, and racism surrounding the history of Persian Pan-Iranian nationalism from its early emergence in the late nineteenth century and the early twentieth century (2013). Vaziri's critical analysis of the rise of nationalism is praiseworthy for its deconstruction of not only the Iranian nationalist narrative but also European nationalism. He traces the early European attempts that resulted in the invention of the Aryan race and sheds light on the place Orientalists gave to a homogeneous Iran in their supposed Aryan world. Vaziri offers a much-needed challenge to the normalized nationalist frame of reference and the Orientalist mode of perception that continues to dominate the regimes of knowledge production in Iran and elsewhere.

Adding to this line of critique that demystifies the Pan-Persian myth of superiority and exposes the direct racist and fascist European role in the creation of Persian Aryanism, Afshin Matin-Asgari (2013) takes issue with the institutionalized and normalized historiography that has been reproducing Iranian Aryanism. Like Vaziri, Asgari exposes the mystifying nature of nationalism in its European origins and the direct involvement of European Orientalists in the invention of the myth of Iranian Aryanism in the 1920s, which increasingly intensified during the 1940s and even after the defeat of the Nazis in 1945. Iranian nationalism benefitted from and benefited its European counterpart, with both capitalizing on a supposedly superior racial origin distinguishing them from their perceived Other or those they classified as non-Aryan. For Italian Fascism, the perceived Others were mainly Arabs, Moors, and, later, Jews; for German fascism, Jews; and for Iranian fascism, Arabs and Turks.[10]

European ideologues of race within and without academia found in Iran (and India) the perfect missing puzzle for Aryanism while Iranian nationalists found in Europeans their supposed kinship, helping both sides to place the collective self in the myth of a mysterious time and place while looking down on large sections of their own societies and the other peoples near and far. In this regard, Alireza Asgharzadeh published a book interrogating both the hysterography of Persian Aryanism and rejecting the fascist nature of Pan-Iranian nationalism. To Asgharzadeh, many in the intelligentsia are accomplices in the ongoing fascism in Iran, whereby non-Persian self-expressions in Iran are systematically and habitually tribalized and minoritized.[11] Anti-Arab, anti-Azeri, and anti-Turk hate speech are not uncommon among Persian nationalists. This hatred is rooted in some old and modern Persian literature and the normalized Aryanist ideology.

The early stages of Iranian fascism go back to the period of the rise of Turkish fascism only with a different path of development. Unlike both Turkish and Arab nationalism, Iranian nationalism drew its inspiration directly from German fascism on the basis of the racist myth of Aryan superiority. Supporting the historiographical research conducted by Mostafa Vaziri, Alireza Asgharzadeh, and Afshin Matin-Asgari, Reza Zia-Ebrahimi also revisits the direct link between Iranian nationalism and the myth of Aryanism in the worldview of European orientalists. One of the early Persian nationalists is Mirza Aqa Khan Kermani who seems to be the first writer who in the late nineteenth century claimed that Persians belong to the so-called Aryan race (Zia-Ebrahimi 2011, 454). Kermani is considered one of the founding fathers of Persian nationalism and is still widely admired by the Persian bourgeois intelligentsia without any problematization of his utter anti-Arab racism, often likening Arabs to beasts and parasites. For instance, he writes, "I spit on them … naked bandits, homeless rat-eaters … vilest humans, most vicious beasts … camel-rider thieves, black and yellow scrawny lot, animal-like and even worse than animal" (qt. in Zia-Ebrahimi 2011, 465). In one of his Letters, Kermani goes on in one of his typical racist rants against Arabs just before making an embarrassingly bad philological argument and then concluding that Persians and the French are from the same parents. He simply refers to the similarity of eight words in Persian and French to assert that both languages have the same origin. Then, in the same sentence, he concludes that the Persian and the French were brothers (whatever that means) but departed, heading in two opposite directions, the East and the West. Still in the same sentence, which, typical of his demagogy and preaching style, is a paragraph long, Kermani tells us that the brother who went Westward "achieved progress, civilization, prosperity, statehood, magnificence, and moral sublime" whereas the brother who headed to the East, the Persian, was cursed by "old thieves, parasites, wicked camel-eaters, greedy lizard-eaters, villains …" who stripped him of all perfections, ethics, and beauty and instead "covered him with lice, ticks, and dirty Arabic cloth" (Kermani n.d., 126).

Iranian nationalism, in both its secular and Islamist versions, perceives Arabs as its main Other but Europeans, especially Germans, as its blood kinship, which has produced what Zia-Ebrahimi termed Iranian Self-Orientalization. By adopting mythical narratives of racism produced by European Orientalists, Iranian nationalists had already committed self-Orientalization, and to make things worse they made every effort to suppress their sense of racist inferiority by claiming genealogical, genetic, spiritual, and cultural, kinship with the greater race of the Aryans. In fact, according to the nationalist narrative, the word "Iran" is derived from "Aryan" and is supposed to mean the land or home of Aryans (Zia-Ebrahimi 2011). Some of this Aryan mythology has also been picked up by many Kurdish nationalists, except those in Iran for reasons that have to do with discursive strategy (to differentiate Kurds from the perceived Persian Other).

A group of nationalist intellectuals influenced by Kermani published a newspaper called *Kaveh* between 1916 and 1922, launching an ideological crusade against all that ties Persians with Arabs (Zia-Ebrahimi 2011, 455). After the foundation of the Imperial State of Persia by Reza Shah Pahlavi in 1925, these and other nationalists became influential in the royal court substantially contributing to the Shah's Pan-Iranianism. At the same time, the German nationalists, including Nazis, provided the Iranian elite with cultural and propagandist support through various means. These included thousands of books, a radio station that aired its programs in German, and invitations for multiple delegations to visit the Reich to deepen relations in a world where the Nazis were desperately in need of new allies to be able to challenge the British and French traditions of imperialist influence in the region and beyond (Zia-Ebrahimi 2011). Three-quarters of a century after the fall of the Third Reich and its mythology, unlike Germans, Persians hold on to Aryanism as some sort of common sense.

Zia-Ebrahimi's illuminating account of an event that took place in 2004 in Tehran sums up the problem of popularized Aryanism. Below is Zia-Ebrahimi's summary of the event after he describes the antagonism with which the Iraqi team was treated in 2001 even after they lost the game and headed back to the airport:

> Yet when the German national football team landed in Tehran on 7 October 2004 to play a friendly match, a wholly different reception was awaiting them. 1,500 Iranian supporters gave the German team a "triumphal welcome," and chanted "Germany, Germany" and "welcome to Iran." The manager of die Mannschaft declared: "It is unbelievable to be welcomed in such a way when you are the visiting team." "I had never seen such a thing" added one of the players. The game took place in the Azadi Stadium in Tehran in the presence of 100,000 supporters. The Siiddeutsche Zeitung reported the "absurd popularity of the German national team in Iran," while the team's manager described the ambiance of the stadium as "incredibly emotional … positive fanaticism."
>
> The Iranians' enthusiasm was expressed when the German national anthem was sung. Right from the beginning, a large number of Iranian fans stood up and gave a collective Nazi salute to their German guests, while others brandished posters of Nietzsche, all this before the astonished eyes of the German supporters. The ZDF TV commentator took notice: "Luckily we only see it briefly, some perverse slips; some people stood, many even, and showed the Hitler salute."
>
> Undoubtedly, these large numbers of Iranian supporters were not expressing sympathy for Nazism or the horrors it committed. Iranians are not as familiar with this period of European history as most westerners. The unusual welcome given to the German team at the airport indicates rather that they were trying—although in an unfortunate way—to convey their sense of sympathy to the Germans. That in the annals of Iranian football this sympathy was demonstrated only to Germans indicates that the message of the so-called Aryan brotherhood inculcated by German propaganda decades ago still finds an echo in Iran
>
> (Zia-Ibrahimi 2011, 471).

When it comes to the racist myth of Aryanism, both the secular royalists, who support the Shah dynasty, and Shia Islamists who support the current regime, are in agreement even though the royalists tend to emphasize it more.

Nationalism's Farcical Promise of Liberation

There is a good general argument about not blaming the victim, or, in this context the minoritized victim. That is to say, it is absurd to critique national liberation movements of a stateless group of people who have been brutalized by a state that treats them as second-degree citizens. Such an argument however should not be interpreted as a free pass for nationalist ideologues who capitalize on the plight of a minoritized group or as some kind of moral exceptionalism visa vie the production of exclusionary modes of perception and oppressive politics. Most importantly, homogenizing any group of people on the bases of national or nationalist identity is misleading regardless of whether the group in question is privileged or underprivileged in terms of the existing race relations. Within racially minoritized groups, there are class and other relations of power, and usually those who lead a nationalist or a religious movement are among the privileged even if they come from underprivileged families.

Because the elites are relatively removed from the everyday reality and life conditions in which the majority of the people they supposedly represent live and because the elites develop their own interests within the parameters of exercising power, they tend to produce exclusionary ideologies that are not fundamentally dissimilar to the ideologies of their alleged enemies. Like the nationalist elites of its rival front, the nationalist elites who speak in the name of the minoritized group end up transcendentalizing race, personifying and homogenizing perceived national groups, and deploying an ethnocentric mode of perception visa vie their community and the rest of the world. This fallback into racism is indicative of the ultimate triumph of coloniality, or colonialism as the dominant mode of perception and as an ideological form with potential overlaps with the fascist form. The nationalism of the minoritized could be interpreted as a transition from political otherness to epistemological oneness, from the position of an othered subjectivity, but subjectivity nonetheless, to a shadow of the colonizer. In the meantime, and within the same process of nationalism, the worldview of the racist oppressor is internalized by the oppressed in a process of *reversed psychoanalysis* instigated by the nationalist ideologues of the racially minoritized group.[12]

Those who do not submit to the regime of nationalist fetishism are often subjected to symbolic, or worse, attacks that even more aggressive than the attacks against the members of the alleged enemy nation. Wherever there is martyrdom, there is much more vilification. Nationalists have a long history of manufacturing and distributing death on the basis of racist mythologies of good and evil. Victimhood may be an outcome of racist oppression, but it is never a guarantee against the reproduction of racism. Both Zionism and Arab nationalism started as progressive movements motivated by the sense of injustice, but as ethnocentric movements, they were bound to become oppressive and exclusionary. Sure enough, immediately after their respective takeover of formerly colonized countries, they became colonial powers visa vie minoritized groups in the ethnically defined and claimed homeland. Some Jewish and Arab intellectuals quickly realized the dangerous trajectory of their respective nationalist movements and defected to become communist internationalists while others defected the communist movement to join the nationalist parties, which are, needless to say, formed according to (explicit and/or implicit) racist terms.

In the case of Israel, Palestinian Arabs from Muslim and Christian backgrounds have been treated as colonized subjects, leading to prolonged hostilities, mass relocations, indiscriminate violence, etc. In the case of Arab nationalism, across MENA but especially in Sudan, Egypt, Syria, and Iraq, the nationalist regimes and militias committed every imaginable colonial and racist act against their racialized Others, or minoritized populations. Considering everything, the rulers of these states and the Arab nationalists in general are not in a moral position to reproach the Israeli administration and right-wing Zionists. Ironically, Arab nationalists started their exclusionism with Jews even before the establishment of the state of Israel. Most noticeably, Iraqi Jews were brutalized as a result of direct fascist politics supported by Nazi Germany. After the mass exodus of Jews from the newly formed Arab states, other minoritized groups such as Kurds and native Africans became the target of exclusionism. These bloody historical chapters may be ignored for a long time, but they cannot be denied.

That said, the point I want to emphasize is my contention that nationalism is necessarily exclusionary and therefore oppressive even if it emerges on the basis of legitimate grievances. Unfortunately, when leftism is weakened, the reaction to a discriminatory and oppressive power is another discriminatory and oppressive movement. One of the grievances of minority intellectuals in MENA, quite understandably, is that in the name of internationalism their identities were tribalized, racialized, and localized while the identity of the dominant ethnic group was naturalized as if it were inherently more compatible with civilizational and universal inspirations of "the nation," which, if anything, is deeply racist, exclusive, and so on.

In 1991, I escaped Saddam's Iraq to the Kurdish controlled areas in Kurdistan, and in 1999, for the last time, I escaped the Kurdistan Region of Iraq as well to end up in Al-Assads' Syria for two and a half years. When I was living in Damascus, I conducted a series of debates with Arab philosophers including two Marxist Palestinian philosophers, Ahmad Barqawi and Yusif Salamah, both of whom were teaching at Damascus University at the time. Ahmad Barqawi, and to some extend Yusif Salamah as well, made a point, that only years later, in Canada, did I start to fully appreciate.[13] Namely, as I pointed to the contradictions of the Pan-Arab discourse visa vie the minoritized groups such as Kurds and Amazigh, Barqawi emphasized that Arab nationalism is irrational, adding "but the problem is that reason is absent in all sides." That is exactly my position today about MENA; the identitarian ethos is irrational and fascistic. I go further to argue that in the absence of a popular leftist atmosphere, most often reactions to fascist regimes do not amount to the rise of anti-fascist movements but rather the emergence of other fascist forces.

Kurdish Nationalism

Here, I return to the case of Kurdish nationalism to subject it to the critical parameters developed thus far in this chapter. Kurdish nationalism is criminalized in the four countries where most Kurds live, Turkey, Iran, Iraq, and Syria. However, the movement itself fanatically demonizes Kurds who are not supportive of it, leaving many ordinary Kurds with no choice but to take a side either with the state that treats Kurds as a colonized group or the Kurdish nationalist movement that strives for repeating the same racist experiment within a Kurdish state.

Recently, in the aftermath of the 2022 uprisings in Iran, citing tangible examples such as the disturbing yet normalized discourse of blood and soil and the popularized ideal of martyrdom, I raised my concern about the fascist tendencies of Kurdish nationalism. The overall reaction only further confirmed my hypothesis. For the Kurdish nationalist elite, their supporters, and countless goons, the identity of Kurdishness is absolute and determinate of all values of righteousness, honor, etc. While Kurdishness designates the so-called ethnicity, in terms of the political filtering and ranking of individual Kurds, complete and unconditional allegiance to an ethnocentric doctrine called *Kurdayati* is deemed imperative. Internally, that is visa vie Kurds, the enterprise of *Kurdayati* is no less chauvinistic than the colonial nationalist enterprises. For instance, Kurds who speak a language other than the two dominant Kurdish languages, Sorani in the south and Kurmanji in the north, are marginalized. People who speak Luri or Hawrami as their mother tongue are expected to speak Aradalani, which is very similar to Sorani, while there are barely any Ardalani (or Sorani) speaking intellectuals and politicians who bother to learn any Luri or Hawrami. There is a similar relationship between Kurmanji and Zazaki, even though the speakers of both languages have been severely marginalized by the Turkish state (for more on this see Çiçek 2017). If we divide the Kurdish liberation movement in terms of left and right parameters, the PKK movement, which emerged in Turkey but has supporters among Kurds in Syria, Iraq, and Iran as well, represents the largest force in the leftist camp. The communist organizations and groups make up the rest of the Kurdish political left. The last chapter of this book addresses the PKK movement, but here I shall pause on Kurdish nationalism or the right-wing front of the Kurdish movements.

There are two main clusters of Kurdish right-wing movements: the Islamists and the nationalists. There are Kurdish nationalist parties in Turkey and Syria too but without considerable militia, unlike those in the Iraqi and Iranian Kurdistan. In Iraq, due to the corruption of the two main Kurdish nationalist parties, PDK and PUK and their brutal suppression of the communists, there has been a rise of Islamism (see Ahmed 2018b). While PDK and PUK historically claimed the Kurds' right to self-rule to be their fundamental objective, and their grievances have been centered around the oppression of Kurds by the Iraqi state, they have shown little respect for individual and collective rights of the mostly Kurdish population they have been ruling since 1991. The Iraqi Kurdistan Regional Government (KRG) is an empirical example for the failure of Kurdish nationalism, something Iranian Kurds know too well if for nothing else than because of the way Kurdish refugees from Iran have been treated by the KRG and the Iraqi Kurdish militias. Yet, the Kurdish peshmerga, the central persona of *Kurdayati*'s hero or freedom fighter, continues to enjoy a sanctified image in the psyche of many Kurds in Iran.

To start to get a sense of the ideology of Kurdish nationalism, comprehending the impact of the rhetorical devices and the central terminology of the nationalist discourse is essential. The literal meaning of peshmerga is “the one who proceeds death,” which emphasizes readiness to be killed for the cause. The word is the combination of *pêş* (before or prior to), *merig* (death), and *e* (to be). Peshmergayati (pêşmergayetî) is the state of being devoted to the patriotic project by living as a fighter, as a pershmerga, within the armed struggle of *Kurdayati. Kurdayeti* stands for the historical and ongoing movement of national liberation from an ethnic (Kurdish) perspective. While *Kurdayati*’s ultimate hero figure is peshmerga, and its sanctified struggle is peshmergayati, *jash* is the antipode of peshmerga and *jashayeti* is the antithesis of peshmergayati, the opposite of patriotism, or the ultimate treachery. The literal meaning of *jash* is a little donkey, and it is meant to degrade the Kurd who collaborates with the occupier, the state. *Jash* is used in reference to Kurdish paramilitary forces who are armed and funded by the state to fight peshmerga. For the same reason, it comes in handy for each group or militia within the *Kurdayati* camp to accuse its rivals of committing *jashayati*, that is, the ultimate betrayal of *Kurdayati* (more on the terminology later as the discussion of Kurdish nationalism advances).

One of the common grievances of nationalist Kurdish intellectuals is that the privileged Persian groups and the Iranian state treat Kurds and other non-Persian speaking groups as ethnic tribes. Yet, ironically, Kurdish nationalists more than anyone else treat Kurdishness as a matter of puritan clannism. So much so, they regularly degrade their rivals by calling them bastard Kurds (*zole Kurd*). Another irony is that they take offense at being called Iranians, but they also take offense when state officials do not treat them as Iranians. Some of the Kurdish nationalists argue that “Iran” is a recent construction by Persian nationalists and, therefore, as the argument goes, such a state does not have any legitimacy from the Kurdish perspective. Just as the Young Turks assumed the Turkish political perspective, will, and leadership, and just as Baathists assumed the Arab political perspective, will, and leadership, the Kurdish nationalists have regularly assumed some kind of undisputable mandate to represent all that is supposedly authentic and faithful to Kurd-ness. Indeed, when they express their views in the Kurdish language/s, they use the word “Kurd” as a singular collective, as in Kurd *wants* etc.; Kurd *was* treated unfairly; Kurd should do such and such, etc.[14] The nationalist takes this singular collective entity *Kurd* for granted and typically assumes a position of guardianship towards it. The closest translation to this supposed entity, *Kurd*, is “the nation.” And, as always, what characterizes and in fact what makes the nation as an entity conceivable is precisely its supposed homogeneity or collective singularity.

Kurdish nationalists are not satisfied with "Iran," but obviously they would have been even less satisfied if the old imperial name of the state, Persia, had been retained. In the meantime, the nationalists deny their fellow Kurds who see themselves as Iranians any right to representation in the assumed political enterprise of *Kurdayati*. Thus, in their envisioned project, only nationalists may be recognized as legitimate right-holders, so *Kurdayati* excludes not only non-Kurds but also ethnic Kurds who do not abide by the predetermined notion of a good, faithful, trustworthy, and honorable Kurdish personality. Those who disagree with *Kurdayati* are automatically considered to be against *Kurd*. Indeed, even within the camp of *Kurdayati* in both Iraq and Iran, every party has been accused of betraying *Kurd* and, therefore, of *jashayati*, by some other parties within the camp of *Kurdayati*. A member of a peshmarga group would be called a *jash* by followers of rival peshmerga groups.

It is as if Kurdish nationalism were the only legitimate or even natural political option for a Kurdish person. A Kurd who does not declare unconditional allegiance to Kurdish nationalism, even when it is suicidal to do so, is demarcated as a bastard, a *jash*, etc. In addition to individual Kurds who do not support the Kurdish nationalist platform, the doubly minoritized groups who are perceived as Kurds are marginalized or excluded from the identitarian frame of Kurdishness. Thus, by excluding the doubly minoritized perceived Kurds and Kurds who do not support the nationalist platform from the identitarian frame of *Kurd*, Kurdish nationalism unwittingly betrays its oppressive tendency and exclusionary mode of perception.

Kurdish nationalism's claim of the Kurdish homeland, i.e., a sovereign Kurdistan, is not any more legitimate than the Persian nationalist's claim of the Iranian homeland. The anti-Persian-nationalist argument is that there are non-Persian peoples in Iran who deserve equal rights, which is of course valid. But there is nothing in the project of Kurdish nationalism, as expressed by its representatives, ideologues, sympathizers, etc., to indicate that the potential state of Kurdistan would be any less exclusionary than the pan-Persian Iran. The Kurdish nationalist elite has never provided a good reason for why we should assume that an independent Kurdistan state would be more inclusive and diverse than an independent (and secular) Iran or for why the inhabitants of, for instance, a Lori speaking city, or any city for that matter, should believe that their lives would be better in a Kurdish state. There is nothing in *Kurdayati* that could assure people, whether ethnic Kurds or not, that a state founded on the bases of Kurdishness is inherently better than a state that is founded on

Iranianness. To date, Kurdish nationalism has not been able to formulate a nationalist discourse that is not inherently racist. Kurdishness is assumed to be a "race," and Kurdish nationalism self-projects that racism in the name of difference, the right to self-determination, and liberation. It imposes the race-identity on vast and varying populations. Those who might disagree with their supposed liberation project are demonized through the deployment of racist terms.

To make things worse, Kurdish nationalist elites, most of whom live in the safety of diaspora, systematically encourage and expect more sacrifices by their fellow Kurds in Iran. These endless sacrifices are romanticized by all available means and the justification lays in the supposed independent Kurdistan state in an unknown future. Kurdish nationalist rhetoric is constructed around *xak* and *xwên*, soil and blood. There are endless references to *xak* and *xwên* in modern Kurdish literature and lyrics, which have contributed to the normalization of fascistic mentality that is obsessed with individual self-sacrifice as the only notion of heroism and eternal collective self-victimization as the only national/list narrative.

Like many other nationalist movements whose cycle of development results in fascism, the Kurdish nationalist movement adopts two contradictory images of the collective self. The nation is believed to be indestructible, eternal, and so on, but, at the same time, it is assumed to be extremely fragile, helpless, and so on. It is treated as a superhistorical entity that has countless external, internal, visible, invisible, collective, and individual enemies. It is typically portrayed as a delicate female figure who is at risk of rape by the countless enemies in a cruel and valueless world. Similarly, defending the homeland is supposed to be the highest honor one could wish for, and self-sacrifice is the only way to achieve it. Indeed, death is the shortest if not the only path open for the members of the poor and miserable majority to achieve the patriarchal and patriotic honor or any recognition at all. For Kurdish nationalism, patriotic mobilization first and foremost comes down to motivating the largest possible number of Kurds to sacrifice themselves without ever questioning the purpose let alone the cause.

The unlikelihood of the actual realization or the feasibility of the nation-state is not a concern for the nationalist elites who seem to strive for something akin to collective suicide as a pathological desire to self-fulfill their worst prophesy about the personified collective called *Kurd*, the nation, as a transcendental victim. They simply refuse to hear any concerns about the actual consequences of the Peshmerga armed struggle even though the most evident consequence has been increasing brutalization of the Kurdish population and the militarization of the Kurdistan region. The national liberation project has already undermined its own claim about emancipation and has become retrogressive as an absurdly irrational movement even by the standards of nationalism. According to *Kurdaiayti*'s value system, only in its loss does the individual Kurdish person's life gain value. One of the ironies I witnessed during the Zhina Mehasa Amini uprising was the semi-religious glorification of death, self-sacrifice. Nearly all these callers for mass sacrifice in Kurdistan were men who live in Europe, North America, and Australia. These enthusiastic male advocators of *Kurdayati* proudly stressed the significance of the Kurdish motto of *Jin, Jiyan, Azadi*, which translates to Woman, Life, Freedom, but they barely let any women speak, and they seemed to be careless about Kurdish women who would lose their lives every day on the streets and in prisons in Iran. In fact, the call for more sacrifice (for Kurdistan) only got louder across the online platforms.

In the case of Iraqi Kurdistan, I have already had that experience, and I am convinced that the Kurdish conflict in Iraq has been one of the most absurd episodes of the twentieth century. In the case of Iranian Kurdistan too I have witnessed how chauvinistic, racist, and violent the alleged advocates of political emancipation can get against their own fellow Iranian Kurdish intellectuals who dare to argue for something other than separation and what in effect would be an ethnic Kurdish state.

Finally, let me share a personal experience that could not be more relevant in terms of its subject matter and political implications. As a side note, I should mention that my mother tongue is Kurdish Sorani, which is the dominant language in the Kurdish political parties in Iran and Iraq. In 2022, I was invited to give a talk to an audience composed of mostly Kurdish intellectuals and activists. Before describing the chauvinistic reaction of the nationalists, I summarize what was and continues to be my position. As also presented in two Kurdish articles (Ahmed 2022d; 2022e), my argument was and is that it is time to have *peshmerga* (the Kurdish freedom fighter) retired politically and figuratively because the armed struggle movement has only made things worse for the people it claims to defend. Sociologically, *Kurdayati*'s hero figure, peshmerga, created a terrible role model for the Kurdish youth for generations at the expense of their participation in urban social, political, and intellectual life. In sanctifying the figure of the peshmerga, the movement has unknowingly been glorifying sheer force and martyrdom while at the same time advocating antagonism against all that is urban, intellectual, cosmopolitan, and so on. The sanctification of *xak* (soil) as the sacred notion of home or the mountains as the core element of Kurdishness along with the mystification of death in the name of martyrdom will only perpetuate a death cult. A movement founded on the idea of martyrdom, such as *peshmergeyati*, will only further undermine the inherent value of individual lives, especially in the Kurdish area.

Moreover, glorifying the armed struggle will only result in further marginalization of education, urban activism, and civil society while at the same time any presence of militias gives the Islamic Republic and arguably any future government in Tehran all the excuses to militarize Kurdistan where most people are already suffering from severe economic disparity and police oppression. Moreover, if not denied the support of the Kurdish elites and the broader Kurdish communities, the peshmerga movement will continue to further the sense of distrust among the larger Iranian demographics, including not only Persians, Azeris, and other groups but also Kurds who perceive themselves as Iranians. Also keep in mind that for a significant portion of the Kurdish speaking population in Iran it is geographically impossible to be included in any potential Kurdish state, which means even if a Kurdish state is materialized, millions of people will be brutalized and probably forcibly displaced. In addition, Kurds will be denied access to most Iranian cities, universities, and so on. Finally, as my argument goes, the geopolitical likelihood of an independent state in Kurdistan is next to none anyway, which means the armed struggle for independence can only result in unpredictable loss of lives and extreme destruction of life conditions for the Kurdish population, who are supposedly being defended by nationalists using little more than old Kalashnikovs at the hands of miserable working class youth who have dropped school to join a struggle that has so far, since its initiation in the 1940s, not materialized anything other than death, destruction, and bad poetry.

I have never been able to comprehend how it is possible for any group of people to have such little regard for the lives and well-being of the very people they believe they defend. Like all nationalist movements, the Kurdish nationalist movement was a product of educated elites before it became a relatively popular front capable of manufacturing endless mythologies, narratives of victimhood and martyrdom, and, again, terrible poetry.

To my written and vocal presentations about fascism in relation to Kurdish nationalism, one of the constant objections was that the colonized could not be accused of fascism. While I do not know of any good reason for such a proclamation, empirically I have concluded that even in the expression of the objection, signs of fascism can be detected. It seems that most of us come to believe that being oppressed and committing oppression are always exclusive not only on individual basis or even generational levels, but on racial, ethnic, historical, and metaphysical levels. Somehow, we are made to think, those who experience suffering, and even more so those who speak in their name, are immune against producing or even causing suffering. This issue is at the heart of the problem of fascism, and without addressing it critically, fascism will always be here or just around the corner. If fascism were a virus, I would say, the sense of victimhood, whether justified or not, is more of a potential cause for rather than a prevention against catching fascism.

The most frequent charge I heard was that I did not know enough about Rojhalat, the Kurdish word for the East, which is used also in reference to indicate Eastern Kurdistan, i.e., the Iranian Kurdistan. This charge, to say nothing of the extensive list of nasty comments in writing, was indicative of utter chauvinism among the advocates of Kurdayeti. I have never been an American citizen or permanent resident, and when I was teaching in universities in the United States, I published extensively on racism in the United States. I faced certain issues in terms of my career and might have lost a number of employment opportunities. Nonetheless, I was never told, at least not to my face and so bluntly, that I did not know enough about the United States because of the fact that I was not from the United States. Yet, these Kurdish nationalist intellectuals and PhD holders had no problem telling one of their fellow Kurds, who happened not to be from Iran, that by virtue of being non-Iranian, he was not eligible to have an informed position on social movements and politics in Iranian Kurdistan. I hope the multiple ironies and utter banality of the nationalist mindset are clear without further explanation.

It is not difficult to point to fascism from without, but we need to comprehend that every fascist movement can be seen as evidence for a fascist environment capable of producing and reproducing fascisms that could swiftly and seamlessly bypass all geopolitical borders, moral norms, and discursive filters. No national or religious group is immune to fascism. The only immunity is the one that must be created through rigorous and continual critique of the unproblematized, celebrated, and sanctified with which an ingroup is supposed to identify unconditionally. In MENA, and elsewhere, if there is any hope for leaving this dark age behind, it lays in postnihilist enterprises that deconstruct and recreate our societal relations and political organizations on the basis of negating the existing forms of oppression. When actual, that is existing, human beings are protected against exploitative attempts that deny them personhood, humanity will have reached a point at which an inclusive mode of perception could also take shape.

Looking back at our age, through a new mode of perception, our world will look utterly absurd, irrational, and entrenched in falsehood. Only when fascism is no longer the dominant form of ideology, will it be easy and considered reasonable to call our age the age of fascism without much theoretical and critical analysis.

Re-Problematizing Fascism: Lessons for the Bad Left

While debating the issue of fascism in the MENA region in English is extremely frustrating given the already existing Islamophobic and racist stereotypes about Middle Easterners, the antifascist struggle in the Middle East will continue regardless of the wrong assumptions of both the right and the left in the West, and those of us who could be part of that struggle through writing ought not to silence ourselves only because some Europeans and Americans refuse to unlearn their prejudices. There has always been strong antifascist resistance in various forms within the MENA region, but unfortunately the intelligentsia of that region for the most part has been part of the problem. The minority of intellectuals, academics, and artists who choose to stand against fascism in their own countries are often silenced, resulting in the complete absence of antifascist critique in the public sphere, except for liberated pockets like Rojava, which has continually been under attack. Given all that, initiating antifascist debates in exile is desperately needed if for nothing else to refute the racist assumption that attributes homogeneity to the MENA societies, whether motivated by antagonistic intentions or not.

Initiating the debate in the European and North American exile has of course its own challenges. The most frustrating challenge for those who are fortunate enough to enjoy some freedom of expression by virtue of living in liberal democracies is the lack of appropriate platforms. Due to the orientalist mindset of the intellectuals and opinion makers in the West, antifascist and leftist Middle Easterners, do not fit in the preconceived image of the Middle East as a homogeneous Muslim society. For the orientalist mode of perception, Muslimhood is a racial identity and race is still a real scientific notion. As a result, for the most part, even the left in the West cannot operate outside the predetermined racist orbit when it comes to MENA.

Ironically, but very commonly, the European and American left more often than not builds alliances with the fatal enemies of their counterparts in the Middle East. Most Middle Eastern leftist forces, activists, and intellectuals, including some of the most fearless feminists, have been caught up in an existential conflict with Islamic authorities and Islamist movements. The norm among the White leftists is to endorse those very authorities and movements. This is precisely why even most centers of Middle Eastern studies at American universities are dominated by conservative, nationalist, and Islamist Middle Eastern academics. Of course, another major factor in making such centers represent the oppressive regimes and ideologies in the Middle East is that many of them are funded by Middle Eastern regimes or rich conservative individuals. Consequently, anti-fascists who are exiled from MENA end up being doubly marginalized.

Middle Eastern progressives in exile face the same problem in publication platforms on all levels. When it comes to academic journals, per the custom, the submitted manuscript is sent to reviewers who are deemed expert in the area. Because most experts of the areas of Middle Eastern studies come from privileged backgrounds or are trained or recruited by conservative centers, critical manuscripts that clash with the dominant ideologies have a slim or no chance of receiving semi-objective evaluations. This in affect reproduces the censorship to which critical scholarship is subjected under oppressive Middle Eastern regimes.

Outside academia, the situation is arguably bleaker for critical voices who struggle against the forces of fascism in the Middle East. Again, because the left in the West for the most part has not been able or willing to recognize the sociological heterogeneity of the Middle East both socially and politically, those who run left leaning publications do not tolerate Middle Eastern critical and progressive voices. Card holding Islamists, anti-Marxists, and anti-feminists could easily use left-leaning platforms whereas writers who are in the frontline of anti-fascist intellectual resistance such as Kanan Makiya (Iraqi American), Maryam Namazie (Iranian-British), and Hamed Abdel-Samad (Egyptian German) usually are not given a chance to publish their works in those platforms. Of course, more often than not, right leaning institutions advance their own agenda by adopting such outsiders, but the left has no right blaming such writers for accepting to utilize those platforms. Of course, the left often does exactly that, i.e., accuse the Middle Eastern critical voices of what the right is normally accused and often guilty of. Subsequently, the representatives of Middle Eastern forces of fascism end up finding strategic allies in naïve White leftists and liberals while the most progressive antifascist voices from the Middle East are left with no choice but use platforms offered by the right in the West.

The same Western liberal and left that fails to imagine the MENA region but as *metaculturally* predetermined have failed to imagine left and right outside the totalized religious topography. The fashionable anti-Marxist, culturalist, identitarian, and post-colonialist mentality has contributed immensely to silencing exiles from the MENA region. Even outside the West, this has had fatal consequences for those who compromised with Islamists or nationalists pragmatically on the bases of prioritizing alleged "anti-imperialism," by which it is usually meant anti-Western-imperialism alone. To take one example, Khomeini was genuine in his resistance to American imperialism, but his movement has been imperialist from the outset. While the Iranian Marxist intelligentsia and movement at large are too well aware of the fascist nature of Islamism, many Islamist writers and intellectuals exploited the anti-American sentiments of people in Iran and among the Western left leaning arenas to increase the popularity and the legitimacy of Islamism.

There is a Western liberal/leftist attraction towards those who combine rhetoric of conventional (Soviet era communist parties line style) anti-Americanism with a selection of postcolonial studies' terminology to spice up what is otherwise typical conservative and imperialist discourses of political Islam. In the Sunni camp, Oxford's Tariq Ramadan is an example of such intellectual ambassadors of Islamism. In the Shia camp Columbia's Hamid Dabashi, the author of *Shi'ism: A Religion of Protest* (Dabashi 2011), has been setting the example for a generation of younger conservative Shia scholars in the West. To dub either of these two figures a "leftist" in Arabic or Persian media would be laughable. Yet, the well-known Benjamin scholar, Susan Buck-Morss, complementing Dabashi, stated that he was "Exemplary of a new Leftist discourse that is undogmatic and non-sectarian," and Dabashi has shamelessly put the quote on his blog, as a testimony of his terrific significance as a "leftist" public intellectual (Dabashi 2024).

Western academics and intellectuals who normally identify themselves as critical of exclusionary and racist ideologies should, at least, not support the very forces progressives from the MENA region are desperately struggling against. If they want to be sympathetic to the Middle Eastern or North African Other who is demonized by the far right in the West, and if they cannot recognize any progressive emancipatory forces in the MENA region, they should be more careful not to take the side of the far right of the MENA region out of pure ignorance. Antifascist Middle Easterners and North Africans in exile carry out a struggle against not only various fascist forces in the MENA region but also against racism in the West. It would be helpful if antifascist MENA intellectuals did not have to explain what is supposed to be common sensical premises like the fact that in MENA, and everywhere else, there is right and left and complicated spectrums of what constitutes relative left versus right-wing politics, ideologies, etc. It would be helpful if more White self-proclaimed leftists actually adopt a non-Eurocentric mode of perception that would not perceive non-Whites merely as helpless homogeneous victims, simply because that is deeply racist despite appearances and has chilling political consequences. It is not that the culturalist mode of perception entails certain blind spots; rather, it is entirely fictionalizing, oversimplifying, essentializing, and, therefore, fundamentally distortive. Culturalism is incapable of conceiving ongoing social conflicts within non-Western societies, but of course struggles in all societies go on regardless of the degree to which they are recognized elsewhere.

Notes

1 The number of Hamas fighters who were killed is still unknown.

2 As Umberto Eco writes, "Italian fascism was the first right-wing dictatorship that took over a European country, and all similar movements later found a sort of archetype in Mussolini's regime. Italian fascism was the first to establish a military liturgy, a folklore, even a way of dressing—far more influential, with its black shirts, than Armani, Benetton, or Versace would ever be. It was only in the Thirties that fascist movements appeared, with Mosley, in Great Britain, and in Latvia, Estonia, Lithuania, Poland, Hungary, Romania, Bulgaria, Greece, Yugoslavia, Spain, Portugal, Norway, and even in South America" (Eco 1995).

3 I propose the term *mobomassification* as a critical alternative to the term "massification," which has anti-democratic connotations. The base term is *mobomass*, which is meant to simultaneously allude to the processes of mobilization of people to make them act as a mob according to a bourgeiosiefied form of politics. That is to say, the term refers to individuals who are ideologically bourgeoisiefied and depoliticized precisely in order to be instrumentalized for anti-egalitarian political agenda (this is explained in Ahmed 2023a).

4 For more on the history, philosophy, and politics of this movement and the ways in which it rejects nationalism and fundamentalism, see Öcalan 2013; 2017; Knapp and Jongerden 2014; Ahmed 2019a; 2014a; 2014b.

5 For a concise but thorough presentation of the striking similarities between Nasserism and Mussolini's fascism, see chapter 7 of A. James Gregor (2006). Gregor is among the scholars who use the term fascism very conservatively, staying faithful to the so-called generic definition of fascism, which is based on the characteristics of Italian fascism. Therefore, it is particularly important that he makes the case about Nasserism's resemblance to Italian fascism. His account of Islamism in the same chapter is equally informative.

6 The Arabic website of *Al-Jazeera* published an article titled "The Role of the Arab Regime in Empowering Zionism" by a prominent journalist who is also the managing editor of a well-known magazine. In his narrative of the main events in the Arab-Israel conflict, the author emphasizes what he considers to

be the missed opportunities of a historic victory of Arabs over Jews when the jihadis managed to blockade 100,000 Jews in Jerusalem at some point during the 1948 war. The Arabs committed what the writer sees as a fatal mistake when they accepted the UN ceasefire resolution, which gave the Jewish forces a chance to regroup and bring water and food to the Jews in Jerusalem, according to the writer (see Shaban Abdulrahman 2014). Anti-Semitic charges in the public sphere are not restricted to the coverage of the conflict with Israel. In July 2018, the Arabic website of Al-Jazeera published an extremely anti-Semitic article under the title that would be translated as, "They Own its Largest Companies: How Did the Jews Control the Porn Industry?" written by a regular contributer (Alsaid 2018). Similar headlines quickly poped up in multiple websites and newspapers.

7 Of course, anti-Semitism here and elsewhere in this chapter is to be taken in the commonly used sense, i.e., racist hatred against perceived Jews. Otherwise, it is well known that race theorists and historians, including Arab nationalists, consider Arabs as a Semitic "race/nation." The Baathists have always been open about their anti-Jewish racism (for instance, see Al-Arzusi n.p., 23).

8 For a screen shot of the front page of the newspaper, including the image, and a commentary in English see, Middle East Eye Staff 2017.

9 The colonized fell into a relationship of mimicry with the colonialists thereby rendering movements of national liberation the continuation of the dreadful shadow of the colonial beast devouring the marginalized and the silenced through means of totalitarian assimilation, at best, or genocidal procedures, at worst. The Pakistani state subjugated the Bangladeshis, and today the Bangladeshi Islamists subjugate perceived non-Muslims and non-Bangladeshis. The Tunisian anti-colonial revolutionary elites immediately Othered their own Tunisian comrades whose Jewishness suddenly was considered to be incompatible with the national identity (for example, see, Memmi 2013). Iraqi Jews, and then Assyrians and Kurds, were perceived as the enemy of the nation even before the British forces left what had just become Iraq on the political map. Yet, in their long struggle to gain their independence, the political leadership in Iraqi Kurdistan reembraced the former colonialists, mimicked the new colonialists, suppressed the population, and persecuted progressive groups (for more see, Ahmed 2018a). Ultimately, the Kurdish nationalist leaders in Iraq used their militias as proxies for any foreign power that needed their services to put pressure on Baghdad. During the Iraq-Iran war, these militias, especially Talabani's fighters, openly and proudly aided the Iranian regime against the Iraqi state, which in turn resulted in Baghdad's treatment of some Kurdish areas and towns, such as Halabja, as enemy territory. Today, Barzani's party, the Kurdistan Democratic Party (PDK) is allied with the Turkish government against the Kurdish liberation movements in Turkey and Syria while Talabani's party, the Patriotic Union of Kurdistan (PUK), continues to work within the parameters of the Iranian regime's sphere of influence. Even in Baghdad, Talabani's party is allied with the Islamist forces that are supported by Tehran while Barzani's party is a member of rival coalition by less fanatic Shia parties. In short, Kurdish nationalism in Iraq has only brought more suffering to Iraqi Kurds than when it was in the opposition. Since it has been ruling parts of the Kurdish majority

areas, it has proved itself to be just another oppressive force by far worse than the Baathists when it comes to corruption (for examples, see, Rubin 2018, and Wille 2020). Also, in terms of the environment, social security, and the rule of law, Iraqi Kurdistan is worse off under the rule of Peshmerga, a term and a figure that remains to be highly cherished among Iranian Kurds, who have had their own oppositional armed groups, or Peshmerga, throughout the last 80 years.

Just like the rest of the region and beyond, in Iran, there was a time when the presence of a strong, confident, and popular Marxist movement stood in direct opposition to Persian chauvinism and in the interest of establishing an egalitarian, inclusive, and pluralist political space. In fact, the Kurdish-majority city of Sinne is still called by some people the Red Sinne, indicating its functioning as the hub of the communist movement in Kurdistan, where communists from various parts of Iran also took refuge. Some Persian-speaking Iranian communists who joined the guerrilla movement even became fluent in Kurdish, which is otherwise almost unheard of given the utter dominance of the Persian language and the endless privileges associated with the Persian identity. Also, the Azerbaijani and Kurdish leftists have a long history of solidarity and collaboration the roots of which go back to the 1940s.

10 For more on Iranian Aryanism also see Soleimani and Osmanzadeh 2021.

11 For instance, see Asgharzadeh 2007, 23, 93, 138, 146, 150–151, 160, 164, 198, 212; Also, see Vaziri 2013, 125, 219, 227, 230.

12 Some of the Frankfurt School's Critical Theorists defined fascism as "psychoanalysis in reverse" (e.g., Lowenthal 1987, 186). The way I understand this is through the classical definition of psychoanalysis as *making the unconscious conscious.* If we go by this classical Freudian definition, then the reverse would amount to *making what otherwise is (false) conscious unconscious.* Also, let us recall that according to Sigmund Freud, "a prominent feature of unconscious processes" is that "they are indestructible." "In the unconscious," Freud asserts, "nothing can be brought to an end, nothing is past or forgotten" (2010, 576). Thus, if we extend the hypothesis of *reverse psychoanalysis* to nationalism, we could argue that nationalism of the minority effectively borrows the view entailed in the nationalism of the majority from the realm of political disputes to implant it in a timeless realm thereby unwittingly and utterly naturalizing the worldview of its alleged enemy.

13 The original manuscript was in Arabic, but I have never had a chance to publish it. However, in 2008, I published the Kurdish translation (see Ahmed 2008). I express my deep gratitude for Ahmad Barqawi and Yusif Salamah and hope they are well and safe. I am also grateful to Dr. Sarbast Nabi for introducing me to Dr. Barqawi and Dr. Salamah in the early months after my arrival in Damascus.

14 Hereafter, to distinguish this particular use, i.e., Kurd as a reference to the collective, I will italicize the word.

4 Imagining Alternatives

Inclusivity, Plurality, and Egalitarianism

The preceding discussion has made two points compellingly clear. First, nationalism and Islamism are extremely exclusionary movements that grew on the corpse of the communist movement, which, in contrast, was the only movement to be so democratic, egalitarian, inclusive, and popular across different regions in North Africa and West Asia. Second, on the ideological level, ending the current crises of fascist exclusionism and its production of violence is not even conceivable without leaving behind nationalism and religious politics in favor of new models based on negating all historical and existing forms of fascism.

Following these two propositions, examining the feasibility of alternative models is in order. Given the fact that the communist movement was once popular, there is no reason to assume that the rise of a comparable movement in the future is improbable. The disturbing assumption that alternatives do not exist, which was systematically propagated during the cold war era and then commonly internalized in the post-Soviet era, is simply false. Contrary to the popularized myth of no-alternative, there are powerful, unconventional, and innovative models premised on egalitarian plurality, but we fail to perceive them due to, among other things, the hegemony of the culturalist mode of perception, which has become dominant in the age of neoliberalism. What is needed is radical deconstruction and reconstruction of the normalized discourses, terminologies, and concepts, thereby emancipating our ways of perceiving the world and enabling ourselves to not only locate but also stand with emerging cosmopolitan movements of emancipation that have thus far been largely unnoticed and/or dismissed.

From the proposition that nationalism and Islamism are cancerous movements that resulted from the suppression of communism, we can infer that imagining inclusive models entails negating all the imposed exclusionary political models to reinvent an egalitarian and inclusive

DOI: 10.4324/9781003351429-4

ethos. This in turn necessitates a radical alteration of the existing modes of spatial production and relations of power. To speak to this point in concrete terms, this chapter focuses on an enclave in the Middle East that exemplifies an anti-nationalist and anti-Islamist project for emancipation. The liberation movement in Bakur-Rojava not only has managed to avoid a fallback into reproducing oppression and othering but also invented an inspiring emancipatory model for inclusivity, plurality, and egalitarianism. In the 1970s, the PKK movement started as a Leninist movement for Kurdish liberation in Turkey. In the 1990s, it underwent a phenomenal transformation that is unique of its kind among all Leninist and Maoist liberation movements that emerged in the second half of the twentieth century. While the movement started among Kurds in Turkey, Kurds in Syria too have had a significant role in its development. In 2014 and afterward, the Syrian Kurds who were part of or influenced by that movement cultivated the Rojava model for self-administration. The following parts of this chapter breaks down the key historical points of the movement and the Rojava model. Hopefully, progressive opinion makers and educators in Central and West Asia and North Africa will start to pay attention to the movement, which has always aspired for reshaping the political imagination and the social landscape internationally.

One could easily argue that there is a radical alternative but most of us refuse to see it. Indeed, there is a movement of resistance that has never ceased to fight off the imposed material, political, and ideological hopelessness, a model that rejects inequality and exclusionism through methods that are far more comprehensive than what the twentieth century models could materialize. Namely, Rojava exemplifies an alternative model that is non-identitarian, socialist, secular, inclusive, feminist, and socioecological.[1] It stands out for its negation of the mode of coloniality in terms of not only race but also gender, and not only political space but also social space, and in all these terms, it is more advanced than the avant-garde party models of Bolshevism and Maoism.[2] Let us elaborate on the roots of the broader movement and the Rojava model to touch on what makes them worth studying as an illuminating and reproducible experiment for a post-nationalist and post-Islamist future in MENA.

The PKK Movement

In Turkey, Kurds and other minorities were targets of Mustafa Kamal Ataturk's Turkification project to assimilate, deport, or eradicate non-Turks, a project that has been shown to have inspired the Nazis throughout the 1920s and 1930s (Ihrig 2014). For the last 100 years,

Kemalism, as the dominant ideology of the state, has systematically turned "Kurdishness" into a source of subjugation and humiliation, compelling many Kurds to conceal or deny their background. Even speaking Kurdish has been stigmatized for generations; a Kurdish speaker's tongue could have been cut for speaking in Kurdish (Üngör 2012, 139; Fernandes 2012). Based on my conversations with older Kurdish men and women from Turkey, often Kurds who did not know Turkish were forced to communicate in sign language in the market-place. Even as late as the 1990s, some Kurdish mothers were not allowed to speak to their imprisoned sons and daughters during family visitations to the prisons because the only language the mothers spoke was Kurdish.

Within such a climate of anti-Kurdish denial, hatred, and violence, a group of young revolutionary Marxist men and women clandestinely established Partiya Kargerên Kurdistan (Kurdistan Workers Party) (PKK).[3] As a university student in Ankara, Ocalan engaged in Turkish leftist movements in the early 1970s, and by mid 1970s along with several of his comrades he became disillusioned by the pan-Turkish and anti-Kurdish tendencies among those groups. In 1974, he and a small group of leftists started a group that would become PKK in 1978. In 1980, the PKK and other leftist groups, especially those supportive of the Kurdish plight, were heavily targeted by the military regime subjecting thousands of Kurdish men and women to extra-judicial arrests and torture. Ocalan managed to escape to Kobanê, a Kurdish town on the Syrian side of the border, and in the same year the PKK started its armed struggle against the Turkish state. Ocalan stayed in Syria until 1996 when Hafiz Al-Assad, threatened by an immanent Turkish invasion of Syria, asked him to leave the country. From there Ocalan went to Italy, but it soon became clear that no European state dared to give him refuge, so ultimately he was driven to the Greek embassy in Kenya, which turned out to be a trap as he was forced out of the embassy only to be kidnapped by the Turkish MIT and flown to Turkey where he has been imprisoned in a solitary facility located on an island near Istanbul. Since then, the PKK has grown and evolved despite being the primary target of Turkey's Western-backed state apparatuses, which include NATO's second largest army (Olson 1996; Barkey and Fuller 1997).

The PKK, unlike many other revolutionary leftist movements, survived the immediate shock of the fall of the USSR, and in fact it evolved significantly during the 1990s and 2000s to invent a unique form of inclusivity that does away with the idea of "national liberation" and transforms "internationalism" realizing a doctrine that embraces plurality and diversity but replaces the contradictory unit of inclusion, or the violent myth of "the nation," with non-identitarian signifiers such as community. Indeed, the PKK movement diverged from the Kurdish nationalist movements by introducing a radical change from the perspective of liberation. Exactly at the time when former communists were turning into fanatic nationalists, Abdullah Ocalan transformed the PKK from a leftist movement of national liberation to a more radical leftist, anti-nationalist, and communitarianist movement.

Of course, in the age of nation-states, Turkey's use of military force to quash purportedly separatist movements is taken as a given, but this position fails to account for a number of key points. First, the PKK does not call for an independent Kurdish state.[4] Since 2005, the movement has adopted a revolutionary philosophy grounded in "democratic confederalism" and Murray Bookchin's social ecology, as advanced by the PKK's imprisoned leader, Abdullah Ocalan (2017). Moreover, the PKK has always expressed its desire to negotiate a political solution to end the armed struggle, and this emerged as a possibility in 2011. However, throughout the so-called peace process over the next few years, Erdogan refused to institute a legal framework for the negotiations, which would have provided some recognition to the Kurdish side (Hakyemez 2017).

In 2015, the Turkish state ended the peace process by launching one of the most violent crackdowns on the Kurdish movement.[5] Even during the peace process, Erdogan's Turkey continually mobilized, aided, and armed international jihadists to fight the Kurds. The PKK, in turn, especially after the sudden rise of ISIS, took its historical and existential conflict with Islamism to another level. In 2014, well trained and battle-hardened PKK guerilla along with fighters from the People's Defense Units (YPG) and the Women's Defense Units (YPJ) made their way to the Sinjar area and managed to save the Yezidi nation from total annihilation at the hands of ISIS (Holmes et al. 2021). The armed forces of the regional government of Iraqi Kurdistan along with the Iraqi army, not to mention the American led coalition forces in Iraq, simply stood by as ISIS carried out one of the most barbaric campaigns of genocide and collective enslavement of children and women in recorded history. Against all odds, the PKK's intervention halted the ISIS invasion at the base of Mount Sinjar thereby saving most of the Yezidis who had made it to the mountains during the days and weeks leading to August 3, 2014, when ISIS took over the Yezidis largest city, Sinjar (for more on this see Ahmed 2014b). ISIS had tens of thousands of jihadi fighters mostly armed with new American weapons they had taken over about two months earlier when the Iraqi Army deserted Mosul, Iraq's second largest city, and most of its surrounding areas leaving entire military bases behind for ISIS.[6]

Another point that is often overlooked is that the PKK was created in the first place because Kurdish political parties had always been outlawed in Turkey. The state has systematically denied the existence of "the Kurdish issue" and banned any political party that dared to demand Kurdish rights. More than that, Kurdish politicians and activists are routinely under threat of assassination or imprisonment under deplorable conditions, which, quite understandably have been likened to those of Nazi concentration camps (Emîn 2018).

Like Turkey, the Syrian state long denied the existence of Kurds in its territories. There too, the Kurdish language was banned, and Kurds could be imprisoned for any act that would allude to Kurdishness, including the simple act of listening to Kurdish music, for instance (HRW 1996). Kurds were also forced out of their towns and villages as part of the state's "comprehensive plan to Arabize the Kurdish northeast of Syria along the Turkish-Syrian border" (HRW 1996, 12). In 1962, 120,000 Kurds were deprived of Syrian citizenship, with that number growing to an estimated 300,000 by 2011, when Bashar Al-Assad finally granted about two-thirds of them citizenship (Institute on Statelessness and Inclusion 2014, 111). Those generations of Kurds deprived of citizenship were legally forbidden from travelling, owning property, marrying, pursuing higher education, or receiving health care. Geographically, of the four parts of Kurdistan, the part under Syrian rule, Rojava, is the smallest and least mountainous. Rojava has therefore always been at a distinct disadvantage. Syrian Kurds nonetheless participated in the Kurdish liberation movements in both Iraq and Turkey, and they maintained underground political parties in Syria, despite continual persecution.

It was not until 2004, however, that Syrian Kurds openly resisted the state through a widespread popular uprising that had its start at a football game in Qamishli, when clashes broke out between Kurdish and Arab fans.[7] Syrian security forces shot and killed a number of Kurds in attendance, and this served as a testament to the state's ongoing repression of Kurds in the country. The Democratic Union Party (PYD), formed the previous year and inspired by the Bakûr movement, demonstrated its ability to mobilize people in support of Kurdish rights throughout Rojava, and the protests that followed had the potential to spark a much broader movement against despotic regimes in the Middle East. However, by virtue of being situated in the margins of the margins, this uprising did not win the sympathy of the majority in Syria and was dismissed internationally. Within a matter of days, in an anti-Kurdish nationalist frenzy, the uprising was brutally suppressed by the Baath regime and its followers, giving rise to a renewed clampdown in the Kurdish regions that saw thousands of activists imprisoned. The international community looked the other way.

By rejecting the nation-state model as inherently oppressive, Ocalan's political philosophy proposed a model of bottom-up self-organization for the purpose of self-administration and social solidarity within and across communities. This became the foundational philosophy for establishing the canton system in Rojava where no linguistic, ethnic, national, and religious identity is given prestige over other linguistic, ethnic, national, and religious identities. At the same time, the canton-system introduced a revolutionary system of education whereby patriarchy is targeted via what has become known as *jinology*, a radical feminist philosophy and a women-led pedagogy aiming to emancipate both men and women from the hegemony of patriarchy and other forms of exclusionism. For the first time in the modern history of MENA we are witnessing a political model that respects the social mosaic and enhances plurality, diversity, and communal empowerment. It is the only tangible and relatively popular model that refuses to create a class of representatives and rulers in the political sphere.

In the meantime, instead of repeating the contradiction of fighting nationalism with nationalism, it rejects nationalism as such, including Kurdish, Arab, and Turkish nationalisms. The Rojava model does not assume any national, ethnic, religious, or patriotic identity, and it prides itself on creating social and political space for bottom-up formations of self-rule organizations while ensuring 1.- the empowerment of women on all levels of education and administration and 2.- the autonomy and protection of religious and ethnic minorities. The form and the nature of leadership is philosophical rather than personal or identitarian. Women's roles are also seen as universally liberating, as opposed to liberating only for women, which is why women have their own organizations and defense units, but they also participate in all the other organizations, delegations, and self-defense units. All presiding positions must be either occupied by women alone or at least co-chaired equally by women and men, which is to say, there is not a single position of leadership occupied by a man or a group of men. Among the mottos of the PKK movement is "kill the man," which a central doctrine in the feminist education all their members are expected to undertake in the movement's academies whether in the self-rule areas in the Qandil mountains or in the urban areas.

The Rojava Model

Only in 2011, with rising opposition in Syria's predominately Arab areas and in view of what rather optimistically became known as "the Arab Spring," did Western media begin to take note of the brutality of Bashar Al-Assad's regime. Weapons, ammunition, and money from the United States, France, Britain, Saudi Arabia, Qatar, and Turkey soon flowed to the Syrian opposition, the liberal and civilian origins of which were quickly overwhelmed by the Syrian Muslim Brotherhood and other Islamist groups. By that time, the PYD had already done significant grass roots organizing aimed at a peaceful transition to democratic confederalism, but it now faced significant local and regional pressure to align with the mainstream opposition. These opposition forces, however, refused to commit to democratic pluralism in a post-Assad Syria, continuing the Baathist politics of denying the need for democratic rights for all, including non-Arabs. While continuing to appeal to democratic, secular, and leftist forces to form an effective political front against both the regime and the Islamist camp, the PYD strategically held back from joining a civil war that had shown no hope for improving democratic plurality, focusing instead on mobilizing the civil society and building up self-defense forces, the People's Defense Units (YPG) and Women's Defense Units (YPJ).

Thus, when the Syrian opposition, under Turkish influence, excluded Kurds from the United Nations-backed Geneva II talks in January of 2014, the PYD and its political allies were sufficiently organized to announce three autonomous cantons in Rojava on January 21: Cizire, Kobane, and Efrin. Although the Rojava revolution had started years before, that date designates the most significant turning point of the revolution, both historically and symbolically. With the Baath regime already occupied with trying to quell the mainstream Syrian opposition, Rojava became the first opportunity for Ocalan's project of democratic confederalism to be implemented without the immediate threat of state violence. The same project had been attempted in Bakûr, but it resulted in mass arrests in 2009, and after being implemented again in the following years, the Turkish army and Islamist militias destroyed entire towns and districts of larger cities in 2015 (Office of the United Nations High Commissioner for Human Rights 2017). For once, Rojava's position in the margins of the margins gave it something of a respite, enabling the movement to set about restructuring social relations on the bases of pluralism and radical egalitarianism as enshrined in their Charter of the Social Contract, rejecting nation-statism, capitalism, and patriarchy.

Ideologically, what distinguishes the revolutionary movement of Rojava and Bakûr from other contemporary revolutions is its multi-faceted concept of liberty. While the PKK started as a typical Marxist-Leninist liberation movement (of the 1980s), it has demonstrated profound ideological change over the last four decades, culminating in a radically new model of life among the guerillas in the mountains of Kurdistan. In addition to abolishing private property and the institution of the family, all PKK guerillas undergo extensive revolutionary de-/re-education on the history of gender and class oppression, socialism, and ecology. The aim here, again driven by Ocalan's philosophy of revolution, is to both de-normalize patriarchal, colonial, and bourgeois paradigms and establish the foundational knowledge for a new society free of domination. Rojava's challenge was to adapt this model to a complex, multi-ethnic, and relatively conservative society that had been under Baathist rule for generations. Added to this, Rojava has strived to avoid lapsing back into statism, fostering a new class of bureaucrats, giving in to patriarchal and tribal structures, and compromising with Islamism and nationalism.

Structurally, the Rojava model is based on a multi-tiered system of direct democracy, the most basic and fundamental components of which are communes and local councils.[8] All administrative bodies, including the security forces, are answerable to the communes, and decisions made at higher levels must be ratified at the local level to take effect. In addition to the neighborhood, district, and canton people's councils, women's councils exist at all levels and special interest councils are also encouraged. This movement has actualized a resilient model of direct democracy, empowering every local community while at the same time connecting communities through shared egalitarian principles and an anti-fascist outlook. It has negated the normalized necessity of the state and proven that societies can be more secure, more organized, more productive, and more successful in warding off retrogressive forces when organized through self-ruling federates grounded in popular assemblies.

Class-wise, Rojava has introduced a successful model of cooperative economics that has reduced social disparities despite the region being under an economic embargo from all sides, including Turkey and Iraqi Kurdistan (Başur). Some leftists who dismiss Rojava have criticized the movement for not doing away with private property, but it is important to note that this was a conscious decision made to avoid inciting violence in Rojava's multiethnic society where the Syrian state had systematically impoverished Kurds and transferred Kurdish land to Arab settlers.[9] As a rule, the movement aims to avoid violence at any cost, except in cases of self-defense, which has become known as the "rose theory" – the basic principle being the cultivation of beauty protected by thorns (see chapter eight of Knapp, Flach, and Ayboğa 2016). For this same reason, Rojava has sought to prevent potential retaliations on ethnic bases and the forced re-distribution of land that had been given to Arab settlers as part of the state's Arabization agenda. The movement has communalized natural resources, such as oil and gas, which were previously controlled by Al-Assad's family and the Baath party. It has also asserted the public ownership of the means of production to the extent possible, without forcibly re-distributing private property. Additionally, there are increasing opportunities for cooperatives and start-up projects, which benefit from communal resources in exchange for a share of the dividends. While agriculture remains the dominant industry, the aim is to create diversified, self-sufficient local economies, particularly given that the embargo limits Rojava's ability to sell crude oil and other raw materials (see Lebsky 2017).

Above all, the liberation of women is central to the Rojava-Bakûr revolution, guided by Ocalan's thesis that women are "the oldest colonized group" (2017, 82). Women in Rojava and Bakûr could be said to be at the margins of the margins of the margins,[10] and given their multifaceted knowledge of various forms of oppression, it should come as no surprise that they have proven to be such formidable revolutionary subjects. The Women's Defense Units (YPJ) is the largest popular autonomous feminist militia in known history, and the women fighters actualize their spaces of freedom through the day-to-day fight against retroactive forces that surround Rojava. Women who were formerly enslaved by Islamists, including many Yezidis, have been inspired to not only fight for their freedom, but also to liberate others by actively participating in the Rojava revolution (McKernan 2016). In addition to Rojava's implementation of the PKK's policy of co-governance, whereby all steering positions must be shared between a man and a woman, and a requirement that at least 40 percent of council members be women, there is also a women's organization, Kongra Star, which leads the fight against patriarchy through a reformation of civil society. The region now boasts women-only academies that specialize in the subject of jinology (the science of women), and as in the PKK, women and men in the self-defense units also undergo feminist re-education. Revolutionary women in Rojava also have constructed the model of the free women's village, Jinwar, intended to address "an urgent and vital need for the development of new living spaces that will strengthen the reclaimed lives of women and children" (Jinwar).

Rojava has defied the typical image of the Oriental Other, while simultaneously challenging the monopoly that the post-enlightenment European subject is thought to have on progressive revolutions. It is no coincidence that this movement has emerged in the margins of the margins, among people who have been subjected to some of the most violent and fascistic projects of elimination. The revolutionaries of Rojava and Bakûr are working towards an alternative on which their lives depend, informed by an experiential understanding of the intersectionality of oppression that is both their burden and their strength. While this multifaceted experience of oppression is crucial to the realization of the absolute necessity of revolution, those in this position are least likely to have access to resources of empowerment, including education. On the flip side, those who do have access to such resources are less inclined towards revolution because of the very privileges that allow them to have this access in the first place. The task for those of us with a relative degree of privilege, then, is to take it upon ourselves to identify with those at the bottom of the pyramid of power and act accordingly. Namely, what this means is that we must utilize what privilege we have for the progressive cause and simultaneously negate any and all conditions that prevent us from being conscious of the general state of unfreedom.

Just when all hope for an all-encompassing cosmopolitan revolution had seemed to fade away, the Rojava revolution emerged in the face of sweeping fanatic and imperialist movements in the Middle East. While continually fighting off invading forces since the beginning of the Syrian civil war, the movement has advanced the notion of liberation in terms of multitude and plurality, creating an innovative space of freedom and equality without precedent in its inclusiveness. Social hierarchy in all its complex forms is being subverted, and this is indicative of the philosophical and political significance of the new revolutionary subject that has been born of this universalist, post-nationalist, post-culturalist movement. The movement has accomplished an array of progressive goals within the blockaded Rojava society that are quantitatively and qualitatively more significant than those accomplished by most modern revolutions, particularly if each case is taken in relation to its historical and spatial contexts. Sadly, given the genocidal campaign Kurds in both Bakûr and Rojava are facing and the international dismissal of their plight, the existing Rojava experiment may not last, but the world has much to learn from it.

The movement remains largely dismissed by the traditional left and of course brutally fought by nationalists and Islamists from all sides and camps. However, thus far, the Rojava model has succeeded in fending off ethnic conflicts between Kurds and Arabs, and Muslims and non-Muslims, despite endless attempts by the Syrian and Turkish regimes to instigate ethnic and religious civil war in the Rojava areas. Moreover, the movement may be starting to inspire other movements of dissent. Most significantly, in the anti-regime uprising of 2022 that followed the killing of Jina Mehsa Amini, the PKK-Rojava motto of "woman is freedom" became the popular slogan across all parts of Iran including the Persian majority cities like Tehran and Esfahan.

While I have not noticed any signs suggesting that the Iranian youth who do not come from a Kurdish background are studying Ocalanism, it is not improbable in the future, especially if Kurdish and Persian ethnic-nationalisms somehow lose some of their hegemony among Kurds and Persians, respectively. This is unlikely in the near future given the continued rise of identitarianism in both camps and the feverishness with which the elites push forward for more ethnic narcissism seasoned with a sense of regional victimhood and international injustice. That said, a turning point is not entirely improbable if multiple events come together at a particular moment. We could be certain that the fall of the Islamic Republic in Tehran or the Erdogan regime in Ankara would suffice to open the door for a significant series of historical events with substantial consequences. An essential point to emphasize is that every day is a determining factor in terms of the form of anticipated changes and changes in anticipation.

Notes

1 While the current Rojava experiment began in 2012 and more officially in 2014, as a revolutionary movement it is inseparable from the liberation movement of Bakur (Northern Kurdistan), which has been led by the Kurdistan Workers Party (PKK) since the late 1970s. As such, even when I do not explicitly invoke this connection by referring to the "Rojava-Bakûr revolution," this shared history should be kept in mind.

2 These models placed too much power in the hands of a few party officials thereby preparing the path for normalizing governmentality. The older Bolshevik and Maoist models succeeded in achieving significant liberation in a few areas but only at the expense of freedoms in other areas. They transformed certain social and historical conditions, but they also militarized the society, normalized police mentality, and brutalized countless lives. Moreover, it is futile to hope for the revival of a historical model in order to transform today's reality even if that model tried and failed to live up to the revolutionary negativity of Marxism.

3 For more see Marcus 2009; Cansız 2018.

4 For a comprehensive history of the PKK and its various ideological stages, see White 2015.

5 See, for example, the Human Rights Watch memorandum "UN Committee against Torture: Review of Turkey" (HRW 2016).

6 It is worth mentioning that the Turkish Consulate in Mosul stayed in the city, and in a poorly constructed narrative, the Turkish government's media releases designated the 49 people who were in the Consulate as hostages (captured by ISIS); somehow and in contrast to every other case, ISIS did not harm the alleged hostages. Throughout the last twelve, but especially for the last ten, years the Turkish support for Islamist groups has only become clearer. In fact, the ISIS episode was a Turkish fiasco, with ISIS itself as a Frankensteinian monster that was meant to destroy the Kurds in both Syria and Iraq and thereby clear up the path for the neo-Ottoman Caliphate to expand its cross-continental imperialist project by 2023 (see Chapters 1 and 2 in this book; Ahmed 2016a; 2016b; 2016c; 2016d).

7 For more on the Qamishli riots and their aftermath, see WRW 2009.

8 For more on Rojava's stateless model, see Strangers in a Tangled Wilderness, eds., 2015.

9 The PKK, for its part, has abolished private property among its guerillas, but it has been even more dismissed than the Rojava movement.

10 Gültan Kişanak, a currently imprisoned Kurdish activist and former co-mayor in Bakûr, stated in an interview, "My own life story has followed the development of the Kurdish women's movement. In the 1980s, I was imprisoned in Diyarbakir prison. This had notoriously brutal conditions, with torture and killings. To be Kurdish, to be a woman and to be leftist created triple difficulties for me" (Al-Ali and Tas 2016).

5 Conclusion

The prevalent order, including its nationalist and Islamist embodiments, is not something that could be reformed because in the first place it is a product of counter-revolutionary forces with deep affiliations with fascist ideological forms. These fascist ideological forms, whether secular or religious, indeed have in common anti-egalitarianism and intolerance of plurality. Historically, since the 1920s, nationalist and fundamentalist movements have never hidden their total antagonism toward anything that is communist and Marxist. This is universally true whether we are talking about colonial or anti-colonial, imperialist or anti-imperialist, movements that knowingly or unknowingly adopted an identitarian perspective about politics.

"Moderate" variations of exclusionary movements are no less worrisome than the "extremist" ones because so-called moderates tend to be especially effective exploiting desperate situations of near complete hopelessness. A movement such as ISIS does not have much chance to become popular for long enough to establish its own state apparatuses of hegemony. In contrast, Islamic equivalents to liberation theology, such as the Muslim Brotherhood or Hezbollah, have more psychological leverage to appeal to "ordinary" people. Once they secure a popular base, their means of absolute terror or total control will essentially rely on populism. Historically, especially in the absence of a radical and popular left, fascism has excelled in exploiting democracy for undemocratic ends. A fascist force cannot become a serious threat unless it secures sufficient populist velocity through democratic means, and it will have better chances to gain populist velocity when leftism has already been demonized, brutalized, and marginalized.

DOI: 10.4324/9781003351429-5

Identitarianism Again

In our world where identitarianism is the normal mode of perception, nowhere is a population immune against an active participation in the reproduction of exclusionism. Any group of people may be able to point to enough exclusionary practices to "justify" committing exclusionism against their perceived enemies. When linguistic structures and discursive devices are mass produced on the premise of identitarianism, ordinary, intellectual, and academic speech become "natural" disseminators of homogeneity, thereby rendering fascism an inherent element of the norm and the prevalent frame of reference. Today, in any political and intellectual setting, it seems hardly possible for people to debate an ongoing conflict without reproducing the same normalized myths of identitarianism. The analytic faculties of even the most educated and self-proclaimed leftist intellectuals seem to be paralyzed by homogenizing frame of signification that is identitarianism. A frame of reference that operates on the basis of nation-statism is far more obscuring than it could be illuminating. Take for instance, any debate around the war in Ukraine, it is virtually impossible to communicate an idea that is not based on the already meta-physicalized dichotomy. It is Russia versus Ukraine, and everything must be reduced to one or the other side. Russia the state, Russia the country, Russia the people, Russia the classes, the Kremlin, Putin, the army are normally but vaguely implied in the word "Russia." On the opposite side, "Ukraine" is used in reference to the entire population who reside within the borders of the state, the ruling group, the army, the head of the state, and so on, with such a sense of certainty that renders any demand of terminological clarification suspicious (of taking the wrong side). In this assumed homogeneous world, Ukrainian Russians and Russian Ukrainians are considered politically and morally offensive to mention. Certainly, the wishes and desires of the silenced majority are considered negligible.

In its falsehood, the mythology of identitarianism was bound to be violent, and through its production of violence, it reproduced itself as an irrational reality. Ultimately, the falsehood is imposed on all, and as long as the modes of production remain intact, the reality will increasingly be constructed as a direct project of irrationality gradually imposing the reason of the unreason on all. When a group of people are perceived and treated in terms of identitarianism, sooner or later they may react on the same basis. When a state treats the population of a city or a region as outsiders or enemies, an increasing number of that population will bond and react on those very bases. In such an environment, if leftism is weak, the popular reaction will inevitably adopt a right-wing ideological form, which could very well be already fascist or become fascist even if it is never classified as such. Indeed, in the absence of leftism, a fascist state could very well produce fascist opposition. Ultimately, we end up in a world where most people, including those who are not part of the conflict, sympathize with a fascist force against another. Even antagonistic camps, in both national and international arenas, would compete for materializing more homogeneity, which is why often even warring camps have in common anti-communism and intolerance toward plurality with each other. Consider, for instance, the deep similarity between Islamist and secular regimes when it comes to their terroristic practices against leftists. To take a few particular examples: in Iran, the Shah regime until its fall in 1979 and the currently ruling Islamic regime spared their severest policies for Iranian communists. A similar pattern exists in the case of Turkey; Erdogan's regime has changed many aspects of Turkish politics, but it has conserved the anti-communist politics of the Kemalist governments that preceded the Erdogan era. Communists who were also minoritized on racist basis, such as Kurdish communists, faced the most brutal treatment by both secular and Islamic governments, in both Iran and Turkey. In Iraq, in the early 1940s, the suppression of the communists and Jews, especially in Baghdad, started together, and in many cases within the same campaign.[1] Also, as it has been well documented, the Nazis started their campaigns of terror by targeting the communists and Jews, so communists who came from Jewish backgrounds stood the smallest chance of survival under the Nazi terror.

Going back to the problem of identitarianism as a dominant mode of perception, conflicts that are usually intensified on racist and religious bases tend to further popularize the fascist vision of homogeneity not only in the hotspot regions but also wherever relevant diaspora-nationalism has a strong presence. Most people seem to primarily focus on the crimes of one side and perceive the crimes of the other side as a reaction, self-defense, and so on. Similarly, in the absence of an international and internationalist front, states are more likely to enter opposing fascistic alliances thereby not only asserting the identitarian foundation of nation-statism but also reproducing racist structures on the international level. None of this should be interpreted in isolation from capitalism as both the dominant mode of production and a world system adamant to totalize and globalize the division of labor, exploitation, and bourgeois hegemony, which would be impossible without diverging politics from class consciousness. The latter proposition can be inferred from some of the important critical theories that are concerned about fascism and/or totalitarianism.[2]

In a Fascist World

To paraphrase Adorno, in a wrong world, there are no right options (2005, 39). Put bluntly, in a world grown on the corpus of an international movement of communism, there is no way out but through reinventing communism in more advanced and resilient forms. To put this in a concrete context, let us return to the conflict that is falsely thought to be the main if not the only conflict in the Middle East. Also, instead of reproducing the false Arab-Jewish dualism, and thereby juxtaposing the views that are divided according to the materialized Arab versus Israel reality, let us pause on the views of someone who is an Arab Jew. There was a time when there was nothing strange about perceiving political platforms and discourses that brought together these two perceived identities and a multitude of other identities. In case the allusion is still unclear, yes, I am referring to the communist movement, including the communist parties in Egypt, the Palestine-Israel region, Iraq, and so on. Sami Michael's characters in the novel *Refuge* are constantly confronted with an emerging identitarian world that splits their identities, fragments the social spaces, and smashes them individually as social beings conflicted by memory and desire (1988). Sami Michael was a communist from Baghdad, where he lived until the exodus of the minoritized Jews of Iraq.[3]

To immune my argument against today's wide-spread anti-Marxist prejudices, the other Arab-Jew I am about to cite is neither a Marxist nor does he come from a communist intellectual or political background. The historian Avi Shlaim is the son of two Arab Jewish parents from Baghdad, where Avi too spent his early childhood before being forced to leave his country to settle in Israel. In 2023, Shlaim published a book expressively titled *Three Worlds: Memoirs of an Arab-Jew*. Throughout his book, Shlaim makes the point about himself as both an Arab and a Jew while at the same time advancing a historical argument to refute today's naturalized Arab-Jew dichotomy. Shlaim is strongly critical of the Israeli state's colonial politics toward Palestinians and degradation of its Palestinian citizens on exclusionary and racist bases.

In the concluding part Shlaim states:

> For me, the one democratic state solution carries the additional attraction of renewing the relevance of the Arab-Jew. The present

> impasse in Israel-Palestine resulted, at least partly, from the central assumption of Zionist discourse, namely, that Jews and Arabs are exclusive and antagonistic ethnic categories. Zionism has in effect undermined the hybrid figure of the Arab-Jew. The Zionist movement was in origin and in essence a European movement led by European Jews who wanted to create a Jewish state for European Jews. It aspired to be in the Middle East but not of the Middle East. It sought not the melding of cultures but the replacement of the local culture by a European one. By its very nature, the Zionist movement deepened the divisions between Israelis and Palestinians, between Israel and the Middle East, between Judaism and Islam, between Hebrew and Arabic. The Zionist movement and the State of Israel have actively worked to erase our common past, our intertwined histories and our centuries-old heritage of pluralism, religious tolerance, cosmopolitanism and co-existence. Above all, Zionism has discouraged us from seeing each other as fellow human beings
>
> (Shlaim 2023, 772).

It is safe to suppose that most Arab intelligentsia would wholeheartedly agree with Shlaim's statement. Indeed, similar critical comments about Israel and Zionism by Shlaim have been widely reproduced in Arab social media and journalism. What I propose here is straightforward leaving no room for red herring or the either-or fallacy. I propose replacing the word "Zionism" with "Arab nationalism," "Israel" with an Arab nation-state such as "Iraq," "Israeli" with "Iraqi," and so on. The new statement will not be any less true than the original one. Shlaim rightly asserts that Jews were a minority among other minorities in Iraq, but his suggestion that Zionism is to be blamed for the Iraqi state's racist politics against Jews could be misleading. The Iraqi state was racist from the outset, and it minoritized Jews and others. It discriminated against Jewish and non-Jewish minoritized communities. That is to say, evidently, even if Zionism had never emerged, Jews, and other minoritized peoples, would have been persecuted on a racist-nationalist basis. The European origin of Zionism does not change anything of the fact that Arab nationalism is of the same class of ideologies as Zionism. Moreover, by singling out Zionism for its European origins, the indictment dismisses the fact that nationalism as such emerged in Europe, which means Arab nationalism too is an invasive force in the region. If, as many Arab nationalists claim, Jews are accepted but Zionism, which is Jewish nationalism, is not, they should also add that Arabs are accepted but Arab nationalism is not.

Shlaim rejects the state of Israel as an ethnocracy guilty of committing apartheid (Shlaim 2023, 764). Yet, again, the same charge is not any less true if made against Turkey and Arab nation-states to say nothing of nation-states that are called Islamic republics. Officially there is no such state as Syria; it is the Arab Republic of Syria. The state in Egypt is the Arab Republic of Egypt. The Republic of Turkey is obviously named after one ethnicity thereby rendering non-Turks second degree citizens by default. Only a Turk has the right to claim Turkey as his or her home, and every government and state institution has made that point painfully clear to non-Turks, including Zazas and Kurds. Finally, are not the Islamic Republic of Pakistan, the Islamic Republic of Iran, the Islamic Republic of Sudan, and the Islamic Republic of Mauritania by definition apartheid states? Given the fact that the minoritized are not entitled to accept or reject such so-called republics, should not the majoritized, unequivocally reject their apartheid states?

For over one hundred years exclusionary identitarianism has given rise to various secular and religious forces with endless internal and external conflicts. Most of these movements started as alleged liberation anti-colonial and anti-imperialist movements. What these forces, from the secular Kemalists, Nasserist, and Baathists to the religious Muslim Brotherhood, Khomeinists, Afghan Mujahedeen, and Taliban, have had in common is utter intolerance for plurality and egalitarianism. Thus, their respective envisioned worlds of course differ in terms of the power relations of identities, but they are fundamentally similar in their obsession with in-group homogeneity. In the name of liberation and sovereignty, they have treated their respective "nations" as little more than herds of sheep. Homogeneity, whether realized through brutal imposition or populist majoritarianism, operates on othering. The othered are marginalized, exploited, persecuted, expelled, and at times collectively wiped out. The century of nationalism started with the Armenian, Yezidi, and Zaza genocides, which are in many ways continuous from Sinjar to Rojava and from Dersim to Nagorno-Karabagh. Whether forced by Islamist jihadism or Islamic mysticism, a political-religious community is a genocidal project of homogeneity and bluntly fascistic. Also, national homogeneity, whether engineered by Turkish, Arab, Persian, Jewish, or Kurdish nationalism is primarily a characteristic of the ideological form of fascism.

Across the region, the brief internationalist chapter was brutally suppressed and replaced by what in my view can only be called fascism. Identitarian exclusionism, nationalist and religious collective narcissism, and the obsession with homogeneity have become the norm. This fascist norm entails the glorification of violence against the othered. As a result, violence and destruction are universalized. The nationalist elites and religious authorities are directly responsible for this war of all against all. ISIS may appear as the gloomiest moment in the modern history of the region, but it was a direct outcome of a fascist century that started in 1915. Between 1915 and 2015, or 1923–2023, genocides against the minoritized continued as new forces of exclusionism and puritanism continued to emerge.

Sooner or later, the marginalized majority from all backgrounds must realize that their tribalist elites must be disempowered. A horizon of new possibilities must be created for all. Racial and religious politics must be demoralized and criminalized. All this necessitates a new philosophical framework of the production of social and political space. But is it true that such a philosophical alternative frame does not exist? Is it true that an inclusive and egalitarian movement is a mere utopia?

There is a continual line of political movements of dissent that has been invented and reinvented by the progressives among the marginalized and supported by other progressives. Toward the end of the Ottoman Empire, the Bundists, the leaders of the Jewish labor movement, inspired a powerful movement in Salonika. Around the same time, Arabic, Hebrew, and Armenian speaking Bolsheviks started a powerful movement in Egypt, Palestine, and Lebanon. In Iraq, in the 1940s, the communist movement, under the leadership of an Assyrian, Yusuf Salman Yusuf, represented the majority of Arabic, Kurdish, and Hebrew speaking people. A Zionist emissary reported that 80–90% of the Iraqi Jewish students were communists (Bashkin 2012, 144–145).

At the End

There are two central propositions to restate. First, the question of freedom is too much for a nationalist mode of perception to comprehend. Second, the basic principles of personhood, plurality, and diversity are outside the parameters of identitarian ways of thinking. Having critically analyzed political, ideological, and spatial forms and aspects of exclusionism, and having argued that the demise of internationalism has resulted in the rise of the identitarianism that is at the heart of the catastrophic present moment in MENA, it is time to conclude this book by a critical assessment of the prospects of hope. The potentialities for ending this dreadful chapter in history and beginning the journey on the path toward establishing a world without exclusionism is not a subject of speculations and predictions, but it is at the heart of the critical theory of society. The mentality that demands solutions or alternatives before grasping the nature and the scope of the crises is part of the problem of the hegemony that should be overcome. Critical theory in the Marxist sense is meant to transform the social reality, and as such its negations are inseparable from transformative and emancipative praxis.

There are two disturbingly popularized conservative myths about our world that can be stated along the following lines: 1- there is no alternative, and 2- the existing world is the best possible world. From Leibniz to Fukuyama, and from Churchill to Thatcher these intertwined myths had been reproduced and disseminated on opinion makers to play their role in turning the dominant order to a metaphysically justified and super-historically determined reality with no hope for redemption.

The problem with these conservative myths is that they do not stop at rejecting radical progression in favor of conserving certain value systems and embracing gradual evolution of life conditions; rather, when they become hegemonic, they inevitably result in radical regression. There are two parts of this argument:

1 Politics as psychic clothing: every potential progress will be perceived with the same conservative phobia, increasingly resulting in the formation of reactionary platforms that compete in terms of extremism as they try to achieve resonance with the frustrated constituency.
2 Politics as suicide: the disadvantaged groups will not be satisfied with the status quo and will sooner or later demand change, but, given the hegemony of conservative myths, which amounts to the same thing as the absence of popular leftism, the oppositional social energy for political change will manifest itself in ultra-right movements and platforms.

The myth of no-alternative, which has become especially popular after the fall of the USSR, already entails the anticipation of a dangerous shift of radicalism from the left to the right. Indeed, the ultra-right has become the more likely candidate to instigate and lead movements of dissent, mass expression of dissatisfaction, and popular desire for radical change. When so many leftists suddenly betrayed their (in) fidelity to the communist philosophy and became little more than grumpling subjects in the neoliberal regime, it was evident that the twenty-first century was going to produce its equivalents of Fascism and Nazism. Sure enough, even in the former Soviet republics, the former leaders of the Communist Party became the heads of the newly established states. The new club of the ruling few embodied a symbiotic association between chauvinist leaders and expansionist capitalists, an association for imperialisms. The term globalism was quickly adopted and popularized precisely to obscure the new imperialist division of the world as a confederation of economic colonies to sustain the totalized system of exploitation-production-consumption within a hierarchy that transforms the racist mode of coloniality to an even more efficient version. Today, the world is divided into special economic zones to perpetuate the world system of class division and special conflict zones to violently suppress, exclude, and, at times, kill those who are deemed to be *homines sacri*, to borrow Agamben's reappropriated concept.

That said, the war industry is by no means separate from the globalized regime of capital under neoliberalism. What seems to have confused former (bad) Marxists and today's half Marxists is that in most of the battle fields the fighting parties come from the different camps within the right, depending on the imperialist agendas that consider war the continuation of commerce by other means. Moralist leftists, social democrats, followers of the so-called liberation theology, humanitarianists, and the greens fail to grasp the fact that most of the wars on which they are so fixated are clashes between imperialisms. The victims on the other hand are the defenseless, unarmed, and brutalized civilians who are falsely classified on identitarian bases as opposed to marginalization. For instance, it is abundantly clear that the pseudo-left, just like the conventional right, conflated Palestinians in Gaza with Hamas. Consequently, they translated their sympathy toward Palestinians into moral support for Hamas, and, indirectly, for Islamism at large. By doing so, they gave the Islamist camps political support and ethical assurance that they, the Islamists, should go on doing what they have been doing in the name of resistance, anti-imperialism, anti-colonialism, and so on.

In places where brutal occupation and mass humiliation of people continue, the velocity of identitarianism in its most extreme nationalist and religious variations continues to increase, practically diminishing the communist discourse of internationalism as something more ancient and more irrelevant than prehistorical mythology. All the while, the Marxist philosophy of critique and negation has been more urgently needed than ever given the aggressiveness with which capital has been imposing its totalitarian space of subjugation catastrophically speeding up the destruction of life conditions even in the most fundamental biological and ecological senses. That is to say, the internalized myths of the best possible world and no-alternative made nihilistic reactionism visa vie the reality almost inevitable. The forms of fascism in their various neoconservative, ultranationalist, fundamentalist, and ethno-imperialist variations are embodiments of that nihilism. Today, the loudest camps of anti-Americanists are in many ways the worst nightmares for the local populations, and the supposed anti-imperialists are themselves imperialists of the crudest kind. The two main camps of Islamism, led by Ankara and Tehran, serve as the clearest examples of crude imperialism, the victims of which are the marginalized in MENA. This gloomy age is indeed the direct outcome of the demise of what once used to be called the "radical left." Yet, at least philosophically, the fallacy is precisely here: in the assumption that leftism is dead, that there is no alternative. A formula of the left may have died, but leftism cannot die. A communist brand of alternative imagination may be dead, but neither communism nor imagination can die as long as systemized social exploitation and the totalitarian rule of capital continue.

As a powerful form of leftism, Marxism is essentially negative, and as such it becomes more powerful when those who attribute positive idealism to it desert it. Giving up leftism, whether the reasons are despair or frustration with leftists, amounts to allowing for the worst possible world to materialize. Therefore, I, for one, am not prepared to let go of leftism only because some leftists unknowingly practice racism in the name of solidarity and some other leftists are disappointed by the fact that communism does not give them what a religious system could give its believers. In MENA, there are plenty of cases that speak to the catastrophic consequences of killing the left and deserting leftism. Hamas is just one example of what the demise of the left entails. This proposition might confuse many traditional leftists in the West, but such confusion is just another manifestation of a deadly model of the left, the culturalist left, which has nothing to do with the philosophy of leftism, as a negative mode of thought and praxis committed to equality and fidelity to the marginalized.

Perhaps, an end to the current gloomy age is in sight, but that would take the courage to be shocked and the courage to stand with the most marginalized for the sake of everyone. Idealism must be not only avoided but also refuted as part of the crisis that has caused so much misery for so many people and for so long. Idealism is not only ungrounded and misleading but also inherently false and, as such, catastrophic when it becomes the normal approach to change. As I have argued in another book (Ahmed 2022a), what is needed is postnihilism, that is, a philosophy for revolution from the perspective of the margins aiming at negating conditions of domination.

Ultimately, the hopelessness that defines the current historical moment can and should be the dialectical ground for hope. The negation of total hopelessness must also be total otherwise a fallback into some sort of reactionism will be the most probable outcome of any revolution, as we have witnessed repeatedly for most of modern history. Negating fascism as an ideological form with endless potential spatial and historical manifestations can only be achieved through a holistic social revolution that breaks free from the cycles of false universalism of capitalism, which has been reproducing tribalism through endless forms of nationalism and sectarianism. Such a negation, by virtue of being total in its scope, as a matter of course must target the material conditions that have been reproducing social relations of domination.

Notes

1 By 1952, there was hardly any Jewish population remaining in Iraq. During Abdelkarim Kasim's rule, 1958–1963, except for the first couple of years, an anti-communist crusade was revived, and this time it became an anti-Kurdish crusade as well, especially in Kirkuk and Mosul, two of the oldest and historically most diverse cities of the region. The Baathists took these campaigns to an even bloodier level while, in the meantime, the Kurdish movement too took an anti-urban, chauvinistic, nationalist, and anti-communist turn leading to today's Talabani-Barzani right-wing enclaves and an unprecedented rise of Islamism among Iraqi Kurds.

2 This is touched upon in Chapter 1 and Chapter 2 of this book in the context of my discussion of "mobomassification." Regarding the direct connection between de-classing and the formation of totalitarian and fascist movements see Arendt 1979, xxxii, 261, 308, 311. This is also discussed in Esposito 2008; Landa 2018; Ahmed 2022a; 2023a.

3 Sami Michael was born in Baghdad in 1926, and until his mid-twenties he lived in Baghdad. I was about to cite his novel to make the point that the suppression of the Iraqi, Syrian, Palestinian, and Israeli communists along with the broader communist movement was the first unfortunate episode that led to today's war of all against all. In search of a piece of information, which I do not even remember now, I googled his name only to learn that he died on April 1, 2024, 17 days ago. He was one of the few intellectuals who resisted what I call identitarian exclusionism throughout his life. The only solace is that he has left works that will survive many generations. It is thanks to such works we learn that the world could have taken a better path and, therefore, could be changed no matter how hopeless the horizon might seem.

Bibliography

Abdulrahman, Shaban. 2014. “دور النظام العربي في تمكين الصهيونية.” *Aljazeera*, July 31. https://www.aljazeera.net/knowledgegate/opinions/2014/7/31/دور-النظام-العربي-في-تمكين-الصهيونية.

Adorno, Theodor. 2005. *Minima Moralia: Reflections on a Damaged Life*. London: Verso.

Ahmed, Salah. 2008. “ناکۆکیی‌مکانی دوو دانیشتن.” *Sulailamiya*, Iraq: Ranj.

Ahmed, Saladdin. 2011. “Return of Revolutions.” *Critical Legal Thinking*, April 12. https://criticallegalthinking.com/2011/04/12/return-of-revolutions/.

Ahmed, Saladdin. 2014a. “10 Things You Must Know About Kurds from the ‘Other Syria’.” *Your Middle East*, May 12. http://www.yourmiddleeast.com/opinion/10-things-you-must-know-about-kurds-from-the-other-syria_23527.

Ahmed, Saladdin. 2014b. “YPG and PKK Forces: The Unsung Heroes of the War Against the Islamic State.” *The New Middle East*, August 11. http://new-middle-east.blogspot.ca/2014/08/ypg-and-pkk-forcesthe-unsung-heroes-of.html.

Ahmed, Saladdin. 2015a. “A Womanless Womens Conference.” *Your Middle East*, February 6. http://www.yourmiddleeast.com/opinion/a-womanless-womens-conference_29724.

Ahmed, Saladdin. 2015b. “Culture as ‘Ways of Life’ or a Mask of Racism? Culturalisation and the Decline of Universalist Views.” *Critical Race and Whiteness Studies* e-journal 11 (1): 1–17. https://philarchive.org/rec/AHMCAW.

Ahmed, Saladdin. 2016a. “From Hitler to Erdogan: Liberal Passivity in the Face of Another Rising Fascist Empire.” *The Jerusalem Post*, February 19. https://www.jpost.com/blogs/critique/from-hitler-to-erdogan-lıberal-passıvıty-in-the-face-of-another-rising-fascist-empire-445397.

Ahmed, Saladdin. 2016b. “Europe’s Compromise with Turkish Fascism.” *The Jerusalem Post*, March 14. https://www.jpost.com/blogs/critique/europes-compromise-with-turkish-fascism-447740.

Ahmed, Saladdin. 2016c. “The Latest Erdogan-ISIS Plot Against Kurds.” 2016. *The Jerusalem Post*, August 25. https://www.jpost.com/blogs/critique/the-latest-erdogan-isis-plot-against-kurds-465982.

Ahmed, Saladdin. 2016d. “Being a Kurdish-Turkish Mistake.” interview by Robert Leonard Rope. *openDemocracy*, September 18. https://www.opendemocracy.net/saladdin-ahmed-robert-leonard-rope/being-kurdish-turkish-mistake.

Ahmed, Saladdin. 2018a. “Panopticism and Totalitarian Space.” *Theory in Action* 11 (1): 1–16.

Ahmed, Saladdin. 2018b. “The Inauthenticity of the Left in the Kurdish Liberation Movement in Iraqi Kurdistan.” *Critique: Journal of Socialist Theory* 46 (1): 65–76.

Ahmed, Saladdin. 2019a. “The Left’s Culturalism and Rojava.” *Contours Journal* 9: 1–20.

Ahmed, Saladdin. 2019b. *Totalitarian Space and the Destruction of Aura*. Albany, NY: SUNY Press.

Ahmed, Saladdin. 2019c. “The 21st-Century Crossroad of Islamism and Enlightenment, Part 1: The Historical Crossroad of an Ideological Crisis.” *TELOSscope*, December 10. https://www.telospress.com/the-21st-century-crossoad-of-islamism-and-enlightenment-part-1-the-historical-crossroad-of-an-ideological-crisis/ and “The 21st-Century Crossroad of Islamism and Enlightenment, Part 2: The Rise of Turkish Islamist Imperialism.” *TELOSscope*, December 12. https://www.telospress.com/the-21st-century-crossroad-of-islamism-and-enlightenment-part-2-the-rise-of-turkish-islamist-imperialism/.

Ahmed, Saladdin. 2021a. “Why ‘Islamo-Leftism’ is Just Another Conspiracy Theory.” *International Journal of Socialist Renewal LINKS*, March 5. http://links.org.au/islamo-leftism-conspiracy-theory.

Ahmed, Saladdin. 2021b. “Universal Discrimination and the Democratic Camouflaging of Culturalism.” *International Journal of Socialist Renewal LINKS*, March 27. http://links.org.au/universal-discrimination-democratic-camouflaging-culturalism.

Ahmed, Saladdin. 2022a. *Revolutionary Hope After Nihilism: Marginalized Voices and Dissent*. London: Bloomsbury Academic.

Ahmed, Saladdin. 2022b. “Mahsa-Amini: An Event in a Marginalized Space.” *TELOSscope*, October 3. https://www.telospress.com/mahsa-amini-an-event-in-a-marginalized-space/.

Ahmed, Saladdin. 2022c. “The Cost of Freedom in the Neoliberal World of Blood and Oil.” *Marxism and Science* 1 (2): 223–241.

Ahmed, Saladdin. 2022d. “نەژادپەرستیی ناتوانێت کەس ئازاد بکات” *Dengekan*, October 29. https://dengekan.info/archives/39241?fbclid=IwAR0WWxJbgv4cBtJAZ_9_HH9BPnnDrik7NBZ9qbP2fiDSLXKeyd8fEjsHMrY.

Ahmed, Saladdin. 2022e. “نەخێر نەژادپەرستیی ناتوانێت کەس رزگار بکات و مەرگخوازییش شایستەی کەواندنە” *Dengekan*, November 15. https://dengekan.info/archives/39392.

Ahmed, Saladdin. 2023a. *Critical Theory from the Margins: Horizons of Possibility in the Age of Extremism*. Albany, NY: SUNY Press.

Ahmed, Saladdin. 2023b. "Fascism as an Ideological Form: A Critical Theory." *Critical Sociology* 49 (4–5), July: 669–687. https://journals.sagepub.com/doi/epub/10.1177/08969205221109869.

Ahmed, Saladdin. 2023c. "'Jerusalem Flood' And Erdogan's Caliphate Project: The Islamist Reconquista as a Doomsday for Palestinians." *Eurasia Review*, November 5. https://www.eurasiareview.com/05112023-jerusalem-flood-and-erdogans-caliphate-project-the-islamist-reconquista-as-a-doomsday-for-palestinians-analysis/.

Al-Ali, Nadje and Latif Tas. 2016. "Kurdish Women's Battle Continues Against State and Patriarchy, Says First Female Co-Mayor of Diyarbakir." *openDemocracy*, August 12. https://www.opendemocracy.net/nadje-al-ali-latif-tas-g-ltan-ki-anak/kurdish-women-s-battle-continues-against-state-and-patriarchy-.

Al-Ali, Osama. 2024. "مقابلة خاصة مع عضو المجلس الوطني الفلسطيني السفير أسامة العلي." *YouTube Video*, February 12. https://youtu.be/YtHuzSfAugI?si=43_nABGywDTd4JIJe.

Al-Arabiya. 2023. X (formerly Twitter), October 19. https://x.com/AlArabiya/status/1715087270208823487?s=20.

Al-Arsuzi. n.d. بعث الامة العربية ورسالتها الى العالم. Damascus: Al-Taraqi Press.

Al-Jazeera. 2016. "مشعل: إيران خفضت دعمها لحماس لرفضها مساندة الأسد" Aljazeera, March 15. https://www.aljazeera.net/news/2016/3/15/مشعل-إيران-خفضت-دعمها-لحماس-لرفضها .

Al-Labwani, Kamal. 2019. "الربيع الصهيوني في دول الممانعة." *The Levant*, November 22. https://thelevantnews.com/2019/11/الربيع-الصهيوني-في-دول-الممانعة/.

Al-Nahar. 2017. *Al-Nahar*, September 27.

Al-Qemany, Sayyid Mahmud. 1996. الرسول دولة حروب [Wars of the prophet's state, volume 2]. Cairo: Maktabat Madbuli Alsaghir.

Al-Sawt Al-Shuia'ai. 1964. المنحرفون من الحرس القومي. https://u.pcloud.link/publink/show?code=XZSzi97ZeQL7li7JT7SCRGpF06IPPkNpgxzy.

Alsaid, Ibrahim. 2018. يمتلكون أكبر شركاته.. كيف سيطر اليهود على سوق "الإباحية"؟. *Aljazeera*, July 18. https://www.aljazeera.net/midan/intellect/sociology/2018/7/18/يمتلكون-أكبر-شركاته-كيف-سيطر-اليهود.

Amnesty International. 2017. *Iran: Blood-Soaked Secrets.* London: Amnesty International. https://www.amnesty.org/download/Documents/MDE1394212018ENGLISH.PDF.

Amnesty International. 2020. *Turkey: Imprisoned Journalists, Human Rights Defenders, and Others, Now at Risk of Covid 19, Must Be Urgently Released.* London: Amnesty International, March 30. https://www.amnesty.org/en/latest/news/2020/03/turkey-imprisoned-journalists-human-rights-defenders-and-others-now-at-risk-of-covid-19-must-be-urgently-released/.

Arendt, Hannah. 1979. *The Origins of Totalitarianism.* San Diego, CA: Harcourt Brace & Company.

Arjmand, Reza. 2017. *Public Urban Space, Gender and Segregation: Women-only Urban Parks in Iran.* London: Routledge.

Arnold, Kathleen R. 2004. *Homelessness, Citizenship, and Identity: The Uncanniness of Late Modernity.* Albany, NY: SUNY Press.

Asgharzadeh, Alireza. 2007. *Iran and the Challenge of Diversity: Islamic Fundamentalism, Aryanist Racism, and Democratic Struggles.* London: Palgrave Macmillan.

Ashdown, Nick. 2020. "Erdogan Wants to Redraw the Middle East's Ethnic Map." *Foreign Policy*, May 1. https://foreignpolicy.com/2019/11/08/erdogan-wants-redraw-middle-east-ethnic-map-kurds-arabs-turkey-syria/.

Bangura, Zainab. 2015. "Q&A: Probing Islamic State's Sex Atrocities with the United Nations." *Middle East Eye*, May 18. http://www.middleeasteye.net/news/qa-probing-islamic-state-s-sex-atrocities-united-nations-1064004421.

Barkey, Henri J. and Graham E. Fuller. 1997. "Turkey's Kurdish Question: Critical Turning Points and Missed Opportunities." *Middle East Journal* 51 (1) (Winter): 59–79.

Bashkin, Orit. 2012. *New Babylonians: A History of Jews in Modern Iraq.* Stanford, CA: Stanford University Press.

Benjamin, Walter. 2004. "Goethe's Elective Affinities." In *Selected Writings, Volume 1, 1913–1926*, edited by M. Bullock and M. W. Jennings, translated by S. Corngold, 297–360. Cambridge, MA: Harvard University Press.

Benjamin, Walter. 2006. "On the Concept of History." In *Walter Benjamin: Selected Writings, Volume 4, 1938–1940*, edited by Howard Eiland and Michael W. Jennings, translated by Harry Zohn, 389–400. Cambridge, MA: Harvard University Press.

Beşikçi, İsmail. 2004. *International Colony Kurdistan.* London: Parvana.

Bouhdiba, Abdelwahab. 1998. *Sexuality in Islam.* Translated by Alan Sheridan. London: Saqi Books.

Boyle, Peter. 2023. "Turkish State Weaponises Earthquake Disaster against Kurds." *Green Left*, February 22. https://www.greenleft.org.au/content/turkish-state-weaponises-earthquake-disaster-against-kurds.

Bozarslan, Hamit. 2014. "Kemalism, Westernization and Anti-liberalism." In *Turkey Beyond Nationalism: Towards Post-Nationalist Identities*, edited by Hans-Lukas Kieser, 28–36. London: I. B. Tauris.

al-Bukhari. 1997. *Sahîh Al-Bukhâri, Volume 4.* Translated by Dr.Muhammad MuhsinKhan. Riyadh, Saudi Arabia: Dayussalam.

Bullough, Vern L. 1974. *The Subordinate Sex: A History of Attitudes Toward Women*. New York: Penguin Books.

Callimachi, Rukmini. 2015. "ISIS Enshrines a Theology of Rape." *New York Times*, August 13. http://www.nytimes.com/2015/08/14/world/middleeast/isis-enshrines-a-theology-of-rape.html?_r=0.

Cansız, Sakine. 2018. *Sara: My Whole Life was a Struggle.* Translated by Janet Biehl. London: Pluto Press.

Césaire, Aimé. 2001. *Discourse on Colonialism.* New York: Monthly Review Press.

Çiçek, Cuma. 2017. *The Kurds of Turkey: National, Religious and Economic Identities.* London: I. B. Tauris.

Cioran, E. M. 2012. *All Gall Is Divided.* Translated by Richard Howard. New York: Arcade Publishing.

Conde, Gilberto. 2022. *Fluid Modernity: The Politics of Water in the Middle East*. London and New York: Routledge.

Conde, Gilberto. 2023. A comment on this manuscript.

Dabashi, Hamid. 2011. *Islam: A Religion of Protest*. Cambridge, MA: Harvard University Press.

Dabashi, Hamid. 2024. *Hamid Dabashi's Blog*. https://hamiddabashi.com.

Debs, Eugene. 1939. "In What War Shall I Take Up Arms and Fight." *Socialist Appeal*, April 4. https://www.marxists.org/history/etol/newspape/themilitant/socialist-appeal-1939/v3n21-apr-04-1939.pdf.

Del Boca, Angelo and Mario Giovana. 1970. *Fascism Today: A World Survey.* Translated by R. H. Boothroyd. London: Heinemann.

Dirik, Dilar. 2018. "Utopia Disrupted: Turkey's Assault on Kurdish-held Afrin." *New Internationalist*, January 29. https://newint.org/features/web-exclusive/2018/01/29/turkey-assault-afrin.

Dube, Saurabh. 2004. *Stitches on Time: Colonial Textures and Postcolonial Tangles.* Durham, NC and London: Duke University Press.

Dube, Saurabh. 2017. *Subjects of Modernity: Time/Space, Disciplines, Margins.* Manchester: Manchester University Press.

Dube, Saurabh. 2023. *Disciplines of Modernity: Archives, Histories, Anthropologies.* London: Routledge.

Eco, Umberto. 1995. "Ur-Fascism." *The New York Review of Books* 42 (11), June 22: 12.

Elaph. 2024. "لدقة تغيب وسط "العديد" و"العشرات" و"المئات." https://elaph.com/Web/News/2024/03/1530693.html.

El-Hamalawy, Hossam. 2008. "Revolt in Mahalla." *International Socialist Review* 59. https://isreview.org/issue/59/revolt-mahalla.

Emîn, Kawa. 2018. "Ahmet Turk Talks About the CHP, Kurdistan's Revolutions, Imprisonment." *Rudaw*, June 9. http://www.rudaw.net/english/interview/09062018?keyword=ahmet%20turk.

Engels, Frederick. 1874. "A Polish Proclamation." *Marx-Engels Archive.* https://www.marxists.org/archive/marx/works/1874/06/11.htm.

Ensor, Josie. 1979. *The Origins of Totalitarianism*. San Diego, CA: Harcourt Brace & Company.

Ensor, Josie. 2019. "Turkey 'to Sign New Missile Defence System Contract' with Russia, in Fresh Blow to US Ties." *The Telegraph*, November 26. https://www.telegraph.co.uk/news/2019/11/26/turkey-sign-new-missile-defence-system-contract-russia-fresh/.

Esposito, Roberto. 2008. "Totalitarianism or Biopolitics? Concerning a Philosophical Interpretation of the Twentieth Century." Translated by Timothy Campbell. *Critical Inquiry* 34 (4): 633–644.

Essed, Philomena. 1991. *Understanding Everyday Racism: An Interdisciplinary Theory.* Newbury Park, CA: SAGE Publications.

Farough-Sluglett, Marion and Peter Sluglett. 2001. *Iraq Since 1958: From Revolution to Dictatorship.* London: I. B. Tauris Publishers.

Fernandes, Desmond. 2012. "Modernity and the Linguistic Genocide of Kurds in Turkey." *International Journal of the Sociology of Language* 217: 75–98. doi:10.1515/ijsl-2012-0050.

Filiu, Jean-Pierre. 2015. *From Deep State to Islamic State: The Arab Counter-Revolution and its Jihadi Legacy.* Oxford: Oxford University Press.

Franzén, Johan. 2011. *Red Star Over Iraq: Iraqi Communism Before Saddam*. New York: Columbia University Press.

Freud, Sigmund. 1961. *The Future of an Illusion*. Translated by James Strachey. New York: W. W. Norton & Company.

Freud, Sigmund. 2001. *Totem and Taboo*. Translated by James Strachey. London: Routledge.

Freud, Sigmund. 2010. *The Interpretation of Dreams*. Translated by James Strachey. New York: Basic Books.

Fromm, Erich. 1965. *Escape from Freedom*. New York: Avon Books.

Gentile, Geovanni. 1995. "Fascism as a Total Conception of Life." In *Fascism*, edited by Roger Griffin. Oxford: Oxford University Press.

Giragosian, Richard. 2007. "Redefining Turkey's Strategic Orientation." *Turkish Policy Quarterly* 6 (4): 33–40.

Glynn, Sarah. 2023. "North and East Syria between Imperialisms." *Medya News*, October 12. https://medyanews.net/north-and-east-syria-between-imperialisms-a-weekly-news-review/.

Gramsci, Antonio. 1971. *Selections from the Prison Notebooks*. New York: International Publishers.

Gregor, A. James. 2006. *The Search for Neofascism: The Use and Abuse of Social Sciences*. Cambridge, UK: Cambridge University Press.

Gunter, Michael M. 2014. "Turkey, Kemalism, and the Deep State." In *Conflict, Democratization, and the Kurds in the Middle East: Turkey, Iran, Iraq, and Syria*, edited by David Romano and Mehmet Gurses, 17–39. London: Palgrave Macmillan.

Hakyemez, Serra. 2017. "Turkey's Failed Peace Process with the Kurds: A Different Explanation." *Crown Center for Middle East Studies* 111. https://www.brandeis.edu/crown/publications/middle-east-briefs/pdfs/101-200/meb111.pdf.

Hamdi, Samir. 2013. "صناعة الثورة المضادة: تونس ومصر مثالا.." Noon Post, September 7: https://www.noonpost.com/442/

Hanioglu, M. Sükrü. 2011. *Atatürk: An Intellectual Biography*. Princeton, NJ: Princeton University Press.

Hanioglu, M. Sükrü. 2014. "Turkism and the Young Turks, 1889–1908." In *Turkey Beyond Nationalism: Towards Post-Nationalist Identities*, edited by Hans-Lukas Kieser, 3–19. London: I. B. Tauris.

Hardy, Paul-A. 2002. "Medieval Muslim Philosophers of Race." In *Philosophers on Race: Critical Essays*, edited by Julie K. Ward and Tommy L. Lott, 38–62. Oxford, UK: Blackwell Publishing.

Holmes, Amy Austin, Diween Hawezy, and Brett Cohen. 2021. "Five Years of Airstrikes: Turkish Aggression and International Silence in Sinjar, 2017–2021." *The International Center for the Study of Violent Extremism (ICSVE)*, August 2. https://www.icsve.org/five-years-of-airstrikes-turkish-aggression-and-international-silence-in-sinjar-2017-2021/.

Horkheimer, Max and Theodor W. Adorno. 2002. *Dialectic of Enlightenment: Philosophical Fragments*. Translated by Edmund Jephcott. Edited by Gunzelin Schmid Noerr. Stanford, CA: Stanford University Press.

HRW (Human Rights Watch). 1996. "Syria: The Silenced Kurds." *Human Rights Watch/Middle East* 8 (4). https://www.hrw.org/sites/default/files/reports/SYRIA96.pdf.

HRW (Human Rights Watch). 2009. "Group Denial: Repression of Kurdish Political and Cultural Rights in Syria." *Human Rights Watch*, November 09. https://www.hrw.org/sites/default/files/reports/syria1109webwcover_0.pdf.

HRW (Human Rights Watch). 2016. "Boxed In: Women and Saudi Arabia's Male Guardianship System." *Human Rights Watch*, July 16. https://www.hrw.org/report/2016/07/16/boxed/women-and-saudi-arabias-male-guardianship-system.

HRW (Human Rights Watch). 2021. "Turkey: Erdoğan's Onslaught on Rights and Democracy Targets Women, Kurds, LGBT People, Democratic Safeguards." *Human Rights Watch*, March 24. https://www.hrw.org/news/2021/03/24/turkey-erdogans-onslaught-rights-and-democracy.

HRW (Human Rights Watch). 2023. "Northern Syria: Turkish Strikes Disrupt Water, Electricity: Attacks Exacerbate Ongoing Humanitarian Crisis for Millions." *Human Rights Watch*, October 26. https://www.hrw.org/news/2023/10/26/northeast-syria-turkish-strikes-disrupt-water-electricity.

HRW (Human Rights Watch). 2024. "Everything is by the Power of the Weapon." *Human Rights Watch*, February 29. https://www.hrw.org/report/2024/02/29/everything-power-weapon/abuses-and-impunity-turkish-occupied-northern-syria. The full report in Arabic is available here: https://www.hrw.org/ar/report/2024/02/29/387395.

Ihring, Stefan. 2014. *Atatürk in the Nazi Imagination*. Cambridge, MA: The Belknap Press of Harvard University.

Institute on Statelessness and Inclusion. 2014. *The World's Stateless.* Oisterwijk, The Netherlands: Wolf Legal Publishers. http://www.institutesi.org/worldsstateless.pdf.

"Islamism." 2004. *Encyclopedia of Islam and the Muslim World, vol 1*. Edited by Richard C. Martin, 536. New York: Macmillan Reference USA.

Jinwar. n.d. "Toward Free Women's Spaces with JINWAR." https://jinwar.org/.

Kajjo, Sirwan. 2019. "Rights Groups: Abuses on the Rise in Syria's Afrin." *Voice of America*, June 1. https://www.voanews.com/a/rights-groups-abuses-on-the-rise-in-syria-s-afrin/4942242.html.

Kanli, Yusuf. 2007. "The Turkish Deep State." *Turkish Daily News*, January 29. https://archive.ph/20130113184410/http://arama.hurriyet.com.tr/arsivnews.aspx#selection-1173.0-1173.11.

Karsh, Efraim. 2013. *Islamic Imperialism: A History.* New Haven, CT: Yale University Press.

Kermani, Mirza Aghakhan. n.d. میرزا آقاخان کرمانی: پدر فلسفه‌ی تاریخ ایران. Edited by Bahram Roshan Zamir. n.p.

Khomeini, Ayatollah Mosavi. 1985. *The Little Green Book: Selected Fatawah and Sayings of the Ayatollah Mosavi Khomeini.* Translated by Harold Salemson. New York: Bantam Books.

Knapp, Michael, Anja Flach, and Ercan Ayboğa. 2016. *Revolution in Rojava; Democratic Autonomy and Women's Liberation in Syrian Kurdistan.* London: Pluto.

Knapp, Michael and Joost Jongerden. 2014. "Communal Democracy: The Social Contract and Confederalism in Rojava." *Comparative Islamic Studies* 10 (1): 87–109.

Landa, Ishay. 2018. *Fascism and the Masses: The Revolt Against the Last Humans, 1848–1945*. London: Routledge.

Laqueur, Walter. 1956. *Communism and Nationalism in the Middle East*. New York: Praeger.

Lebsky, Maksim. 2017. "The Economy of Rojava." *Co-operative Economy*, March 14. https://cooperativeeconomy.info/the-economy-of-rojava/.

Lefebvre, Henri. 1991. *The Production of Space.* Translated by Donald Nicholson-Smith. Malden, MA: Blackwell Publishing.

Lenin, V. I. 1965. *Lenin's Collected Works Volume 28*, 78–83. Translated and edited by Jim Riordan. Moscow: Progress Publishers. https://www.marxists.org/archive/lenin/works/1918/aug/23a.htm.

Lenin, V. I. 2005. "Speech Delivered at an International Meeting in Berne, February 8, 1916." *Marxist Internet Archive.* https://www.marxists.org/archive/lenin/works/1916/feb/08.htm#fwV22E030.

Lowenthal, Leo. 1987. *An Unmastered Past: The Autobiographical Reflections of Leo Lowenthal*. Berkely, CA: University of California Press.

Marcus, Aliza. 2009. *Blood and Belief: The PKK and the Kurdish Fight for Independence.* New York: New York University Press.

Matin-Asgari, Afshin. 2018. *Both Eastern and Western: An Intellectual History of Iranian Modernity.* Cambridge, UK: Cambridge University Press.

McKernan, Bethan. 2016. "All-female Yazidi Militia Launches Operation for Revenge on ISIS in Northern Iraq." *The Independent*, November 14.

Memmi, Albert. 2013. *The Pillar of Salt*. Lexington, MA: Plunkett Lake Press.

Michael, Sami. 1988. *Refuge.* Translated by Edward Crossman. Philadelphia, PA: Jewish Publication Society.

Middle East Eye Staff. 2017. "'Disgusting': Iraqi Paper Depicts Kurdistan as Woman Facing Rape." *Middle East Eye*, September 29. https://www.middleeasteye.net/news/disgusting-iraqi-paper-depicts-kurdistan-woman-facing- rape.

Mikhail, Alan. 2020. *God's Shadow: Sultan Selim, His Ottoman Empire, and the Making of the Modern World.* New York: Liveright.

Mikhail, Alan. 2021. *God's Shadow: The Ottoman Sultan Who Shaped the Modern World.* London: Faber & Faber.

Öcalan, Abdullah. 2013. *Liberating Life: Woman's Revolution*. Cologne, Germany: International Initiative Edition. https://www.freeocalan.org/wp-content/uploads/2014/06/liberating-Lifefinal.pdf.

Öcalan, Abdullah. 2017. *The Political Thought of Abdullah Öcalan: Kurdistan, Women's Revolution and Democratic Confederalism*. Translated by Havin Güneşer. London: Pluto Press.

Office of the United Nations High Commissioner for Human Rights. 2017. https://digitallibrary.un.org/record/1474804?v=pdf.

Olson, Robert. 1996. "The Kurdish Question and Turkey's Foreign Policy toward Syria, Iran, Russia and Iraq Since the Gulf War." In *The Kurdish*

Nationalist Movement in the 1990s: Its Impact on Turkey and the Middle East, edited by Robert Olson, 84–112. Lexington, KY: The University Press of Kentucky.

Oxfam. 2022. "Profiting from Pain: Oxfam Media Briefing." *Oxfam International*, May 23. https://www.oxfam.org/en/research/profiting-pain.

Quijano, Anibal. 2000. "Coloniality of Power and Eurocentrism in Latin America." *Nepantla: Views from South* 1 (3): 533–580.

Reich, Wilhelm. 1970. *The Mass Psychology of Fascism*. Edited by Mary Higgins and Chester M. Raphael. New York: Farrar, Straus and Giroux.

Rodney, Walter. 2018. *How Europe Underdeveloped Africa*. London: Verso.

Rubin, Michael. 2018. "The Continuing Problem of KRG Corruption." In *Routledge Handbook on the Kurds*, edited by M. Gunter, chapter 12. London: Routledge. doi:10.4324/9781315627427.

Said, Edward. 2000. *Reflections on Exile and Other Essays*. Cambridge, MA: Harvard University Press.

Şen, Dilek. 2021. "Though we Call it 'Deep,' This is the State Structure Established in our Geography." *Bianet English*, June 2. https://bianet.org/haber/though-we-call-it-deep-this-is-the-state-structure-established-in-our-geography-245058.

Shlaim, Avi. 2023. *Three Worlds: Memoirs of an Arab-Jew*. London: Oneworld Publications.

Soleimani, Kamal and Davoud Osmanzadeh. 2021. "Textualising the Ethno-religious Sovereign, History, Ethnicity and Nationalism in the Perso-Islamic Textbooks." *Nations & Nationalism* 28 (2). doi:10.1111/nana.12705.

Strangers in a Tangled Wilderness, eds. 2015. *A Small Key Can Open a Large Door: The Rojava Revolution*. United States: Strangers in a Tangled Wilderness.

Ter-Matevosyan, Vahram. 2015. "Turkish Experience with Totalitarianism and Fascism: Tracing the Intellectual Origins." *Iran and the Caucasus* 19 (4): 387–401.

Tibi, Bassam. 1997. *Arab Nationalism: Between Islam and the Nation-State*. New York, NY: St. Martin's Press.

Tibi, Basam. 2012. *Islamism and Islam*. New Haven, CT: Yale University Press.

Torchia, Christopher. 2007. "Old Question Revisited After Journo's Murder." *IOL*, February 1. https://www.iol.co.za/news/world/old-question-revisited-after-journos-murder-313454.

Trotsky, Leon. 1939. "Only Revolution Can Put an End to War." *Socialist Appeal*, April 4. Accessed April 12, 2022. https://www.marxists.org/history/etol/newspape/themilitant/socialist-appeal-1939/v3n21-apr-04-1939.pdf.

TRT. 2023. "الاستخبارات التركية تنقذ مطور برمجيات فلسطينياً من يد الموساد" *YouTube Video*, November 22. https://youtu.be/u7d6KCzjR6g?si=1jSw5uX8hpF7xpRj.

Üngör, Uğur Ümit. 2012. "Untying the Tongue-Tied: Ethnocide and Language Politics." *International Journal of the Sociology of Language* 217: 127–150. https://doi.org.proxy.lib.umich.edu/10.1515/ijsl-2012-0052.

Vaziri, Mostafa. 2013. *Iran as Imagined Nation: The Construction of National Identity.* New Jersey: Gorgias Press. (Original publication New York: Paragon House, 1993).

Yaseen, Abdulkadir. 2011. الحركة الشيوعية المصرية: الجذور - القسمات - المال ١٩٢١-١٩٦٥ *[The Egyptian Communist Movement: The Roots, the Divisions, the Finance 1921–1965].* Cairo: The Egyptian Public Institution for Books.

White, Paul. 2015. *The PKK: Coming Down from the Mountains.* London: Zed Books.

Wille, Belkis. 2020. "The KRG Needs to Listen to Critics, Not Arrest Them." *Human Rights Watch*, June 15. https://www.hrw.org/news/2020/06/15/krg-needs-listen-critics-not-arrest-them.

Zia-Ebrahimi, Reza. 2011. "Self-Orientalization and Dislocation: The Uses and Abuses of the 'Aryan' Discourse in Iran." *Iranian Studies* 44 (4): 445–472.

Žižek, Slavoj. 2008. *In Defence of Lost Causes.* London: Verso Books.

Index

For Product Safety Concerns and Information please contact our EU representative GPSR@taylorandfrancis.com
Taylor & Francis Verlag GmbH, Kaufingerstraße 24, 80331 München, Germany

www.ingramcontent.com/pod-product-compliance
Lightning Source LLC
LaVergne TN
LVHW010950110826
845149LV00015B/3291

* 9 7 8 1 0 3 2 3 9 8 0 1 3 *